THE ARCHITECT AND SOCIETY
EDITED BY
JOHN FLEMING AND HUGH HONOUR

Hans Aurenhammer

J.B. Fischer von Erlach

ALLEN LANE

Copyright © Hans Aurenhammer, 1973
First published in Great Britain in 1973

Allen Lane
A Division of Penguin Books Ltd
21 John Street, London WC1N 2BT

ISBN 0 7139 0440 2

Set in Monophoto Garamond by
Oliver Burridge Filmsetting Ltd, Crawley
Printed by Butler and Tanner Ltd,
Frome, Somerset
Designed by Gerald Cinamon

TO OTTO DEMUS

Contents

List of Illustrations

(All photographs courtesy Bildarchiv der Österreichischen Nationalbibliothek unless credited otherwise)

Foreword

A series of exhibitions were held in various towns in Austria, Germany, and Switzerland in 1956 and 1957 to commemorate the three hundredth anniversary of the birth of Johann Bernhard Fischer von Erlach. The occasion was also marked by the publication of a comprehensive monograph and of several other scholarly works devoted to the architect and his work. Despite this, relatively little interest was aroused in the English-speaking world where, it would seem, Fischer has yet to be accorded the place that he deserves as an architect of truly European stature.

I should therefore like to thank the editors of this series of books, John Fleming and Hugh Honour, most sincerely for giving me the opportunity of re-introducing Fischer and his work to the English-speaking public. What is more, the sociological aspect of the series provides a very useful opportunity for reviewing the architect's achievements in the light of the social and political climate of the period in which he was living and working, that is, as architecture which reflected the rise of the Habsburg Empire to the status of a European power. In so doing, I hope to make some contribution towards a better understanding of the Austrian Baroque – a style in art and architecture which Fischer inaugurated.

Fischer had several connections with England. He visited London in 1704 and his later works provide indisputable evidence of his close study of English architecture during that visit. After the period of copyright had elapsed, his great history of architecture was reprinted in London in 1730 and very soon afterwards appeared in a second impression. A renewal of interest in Baroque art in the 1920s resulted in the publication in 1924 of an English work on Fischer by H. V. Lanchester, in the series 'Masters of Architecture', but so far no English monograph has taken account of all the most recent research. It is my hope that this book will to some extent remedy this deficiency. I cannot, of course, go into all the details, which would in any case be of little interest to readers outside Austria, but I shall try to show especially how Fischer's distinctive qualities as an architect striving for universality were reflected in his most important works.

Finally, I should like to thank everyone who has helped me in the writing of this book and most of all my wife, without whose support and encouragement it would never have been completed.

·1·
Fischer
and his Time

How was it possible for Austria, and above all Vienna, after having been virtually an Italian province in the realm of art and architecture for almost two centuries, to become suddenly, at the end of the seventeenth century, a focal point of artistic achievement once more? How was it possible for this to have happened as the result of the work of one man? Was it simply because of the universal artistic genius of this one individual or was it rather because of the happy coincidence of an outstanding architect with a social and political situation which called for impressive buildings? Great architecture has always represented and expressed great power. The most brilliant architectonic gifts are bound to wither away if the architect does not receive important commissions. It was Fischer's good fortune that he was born at the right time and in the right country, that his education as an architect was universal, and that he found congenial patrons and suitable commissions which enabled him to exploit his ideas to the full.

After the Thirty Years' War (1618–48), the Emperor's position within the Holy Roman Empire was very weak indeed. The German princes enjoyed complete political freedom. The Empire had become little more than a loose federation of states, held together by the election and the person of the Emperor, the imperial diets and the imperial courts of justice. The Emperor could only maintain his position by means of his 'domestic power', that is to say, by using the power of the inherited Habsburg countries. The Emperor's position within the Empire had been weakened, after the peace treaties concluded at the end of the Thirty Years' War, by the privileges granted to the princes of the Empire. At the same time, this fact served to strengthen his position in the Austrian countries which he himself ruled as prince. It was at this time that changes were made in the constitutions of Lower and Upper Austria, Styria, Carinthia, Carniola, the Tyrol, Silesia, Bohemia,

Moravia and Hungary. As a result the three 'estates' of these countries lost more and more of their privileges and an absolute Habsburg state began gradually but unmistakably to emerge. The Emperor, who always had to be prepared to go to war, kept a standing army at his disposal. Religious unity had been almost completely restored in the Habsburg countries, where the Counter-Reformation was still going on, propagated by the religious orders, strengthening the Catholic faith, and almost totally wiping out the remnants of Protestantism. The consequence of all this was that the ruling family came to regard the idea of a Habsburg Empire as more important than that of the Holy Roman Empire.

During the Thirty Years' War, there had been peace on the eastern frontier of the Empire. The Turks, who had besieged Vienna in 1529 but had then been compelled to withdraw, had not changed their position in the Balkans since the peace of 1606. The wars against the Turks did not recommence until 1663. The Emperor, Leopold I (1658–1705), was obliged to wage war on two fronts. In the west, he had to defend the inwardly divided German Empire against the attacks of the French. Louis XIV, anxious to obtain supremacy in Europe, supported the Turks and the Hungarian rebels from time to time in their struggle against the Emperor. The Turkish advance of 1683 on Vienna undoubtedly constituted the greatest threat to central Europe, but the Emperor succeeded in assembling a powerful striking force. He found a strong ally in John III Sobieski, the King of Poland. Military aid was supplied by the Electors of Bavaria and Saxony and by several other less notable princes of the Empire. Pope Innocent XI gave financial assistance, as did Savoy, Tuscany, Genoa, Spain and Portugal. Although Vienna was defended heroically by its soldiers and citizens, who suffered from famine and disease during the siege, the city would not have been able to withstand the Turks if it had not been relieved, after a siege of two months, by the imperial army and the troops of the Emperor's Polish ally. This vigorous engagement resulted in the liberation of Vienna and in the pursuit of the Turks deep into Hungary. The defeat prevented the Turks from penetrating any farther into central Europe.

The Emperor continued the war in the hope of annihilating the hitherto constant threat to central Europe and of thwarting French policy. In 1684 he concluded a treaty with the Pope, Venice, and Poland, setting up the so-called Holy League. The troops fighting against the Turks in Hungary under the command of Duke Charles of Lorraine were consistently victorious. Louis XIV's ruthless annexation of German territory resulted in uniting the German princes of the Empire and in bringing them closer to the Emperor than they had been for a long time. In 1689 England and the

Netherlands concluded the Grand Alliance with the Emperor against Louis XIV. After the Peace of Rijswijk in 1697, it was obvious that the Sun King had not been able to achieve French supremacy in central Europe and that the power of the Emperor had been greatly increased. It was in 1697 too that Leopold I made Prince Eugene of Savoy commander-in-chief of the imperial army in Hungary. Prince Eugene, the most important military leader in Austrian history, was also to become one of the most influential ministers at the imperial court. After his decisive victory over the Turks, peace was concluded in 1699 and the Emperor gained control over the whole of Hungary, Transylvania, and a large part of Slavonia. The Habsburgs thus came to possess a large and well-defined territory, the eastern frontier of which seemed to be quite safe from attack. From 1683 onwards, after the victory over the Turks and after having averted the danger of the French claim to supremacy in central Europe, Austria was a great power. Leopold I had succeeded in restoring the glory to imperial power, which had been so weak after the end of the Thirty Years' War.

Whereas the conflict with France had only indirectly affected the Austrian lands, the Turkish invasion of 1683 left deep wounds in Lower Austria, Styria and Hungary. The Turks had put to death great numbers of people in the towns and villages in the most brutal way, or they had deported them, sold them as slaves, and burnt their homes. When there was no longer any danger from the Turks, those who had managed to escape were faced with the immense task of rebuilding. The devastated lands had to be restored and even partly recolonized. In addition, the plague had reached Austria from Hungary by 1679 and this had depopulated the country even before the Turks had invaded it. New settlers from the Alpine districts and from southern and central Germany now came to cultivate the soil of Lower Austria and Styria. In Hungary recolonization was carefully controlled by the authorities, with the result that all the lands that had been laid waste or neglected during the long Turkish occupation and during the war against the Turks were rapidly transformed into prosperous and fruitful countryside. The Emperor's victories and an increasing feeling of security among the people did more than anything else to encourage recultivation and rebuilding. The visible result of the restoration of Catholicism, of the renewal of the imperial ideal and the rise of Austria to the level of a great power, was a sudden flowering of art and architecture – patronized by the Emperor, the Church and the nobility, but also affecting the townsmen. Suddenly, the whole country seemed to take on a new appearance.

It would be misleading to suggest that the Thirty Years' War and its aftermath had led to a complete suppression of the arts in

Austria during the seventeenth century. There were, in fact, some art centres of local importance which had grown up around the residences of the Landesfürsten, these towns also being the most active centres of the Counter-Reformation. The division of the Habsburg lands between the three sons of Emperor Ferdinand I in 1554 had resulted in the emergence of three separate zones, each with its own residence. These residences were situated in Vienna, Graz and Innsbruck. (It was, incidentally, not until the reign of Leopold I that all the Habsburg patrimonial dominions were reunited.) Another important centre of culture, art and learning was the Archbishop's court at Salzburg. At a time when the axiom *Cuius regio eius religio* prevailed the Counter-Reformation was in fact carried out by the government. It was, however, accompanied by a renewal of religious life, zealously promoted by the Church. The religious orders made a very important contribution to this work of renewal, especially in the sphere of education and science. In the various conventual houses, great encouragement was given to the arts as a means of propagating the Catholic faith.

Until about 1680 art in the Habsburg countries was almost entirely dependent on those countries which had brought the Counter-Reformation to Austria, in other words, Italy, the Spanish Netherlands, and southern Germany. Itinerant artists from these countries lived and worked at the courts and in the monasteries. Whole families of architects, stucco workers, sculptors and painters from Upper Italy were employed, one generation often following another. Some of them had already settled in Austria. Their work was more often executed in the style of Italian Mannerism than in that of the Early Baroque. Looked at from the point of view of Europe as a whole, Austria was certainly on the fringe of artistic development. The centres of dynamic artistic creation were Rome, Paris, and London. During the first three quarters of the seventeenth century, the artistic achievements of Austria were undeniably behind the times. In addition to the court artists and architects, there were also craftsmen, in particular wood-carvers, working in a tradition which went back to the late Middle Ages. However, apart from a few notable Italianate buildings – spacious churches and monasteries built in a style combining Mannerist and Early Baroque features and richly decorated with stucco by Italian craftsmen – seventeenth-century Austrian architecture up to the time of the Turkish invasion not only lacked unity, but also the impulse to create a style of its own.

Johann Bernhard Fischer was born in Graz, one of the local centres of artistic activity in Austria, and baptized in the parish church of the Heiliges Blut on 20 July 1656. Both his parents came from notable Graz 'Bürger' families. His father was a turner and sculptor and his grandfather had been a bookseller. His mother was the daughter of a joiner and had also been the wife of a sculptor, Sebastian Erlacher, before her second marriage. It was customary in those days for a man to marry the widow of a fellow-member of his own guild, in whose workshop he had been trained and had worked as a journeyman. The number of masters practising a given trade in any town was limited, even in the seventeenth century, by the medieval guild laws; and it often happened that the only way for a journeyman to be accepted by his guild as a master was by marrying a master's widow and taking over his workshop. That is exactly what Fischer's father had done.

The family may originally have been Dutch. Certainly Fischer's son, Joseph Emanuel Fischer von Erlach, when applying for a barony, named as his ancestor one Peter de Vischer, counsellor to the Archduke Albert, the Habsburg Regent of the Spanish Netherlands (1595–1621). But it need hardly be said that such attempts to prove noble ancestry do not always have to be taken too seriously.

In any event, the young Fischer grew up in the tradition of Styrian craftsmanship and in an environment of quite important architectural achievements. At this time Graz was no longer a Habsburg residence, but the buildings of the court, the Styrian government and the most important Styrian family, the Princes of Eggenberg, recalled the period in which the north Italian Mannerist style had been introduced by Italian artists and architects. As a centre of the Counter-Reformation and of artistic influence, the city had been of greater importance than the other two Habsburg residences. When the Archduke of Styria had become Emperor Ferdinand II in 1619, Graz had at once lost its pre-eminent position as a residence. But the local government, the so-called 'states' of Styria represented at the diet, and the local nobility – especially the Princes of Eggenberg – tried to take over the role of the dynasty as patrons of the arts. Native craftsmen, organized in guilds and subject to their laws, worked in Graz alongside the Italian artists. Among them was Fischer's father, Johann Baptist Fischer. He is known to have been one of the craftsmen who contributed to the interior decoration of the Landhaus in Graz, the seat of the Styrian local government, and to the sculptural decorations of the castle of the Eggenberg family near Graz. He also carved statues for Styrian village churches. As a sculptor, he followed the good tradition of Styrian craftsmanship, but his work was undeniably provincial in character. There can be no doubt that it was in his workshop that Fischer, the future architect, received his early training as a turner and sculptor.

Although Fischer came from a provincial town and was brought up in a restricted social and artistic environment, he overcame this handicap through his long stay in Italy. It was quite usual at this time for young and ambitious Austrian artists to go to Italy, but Fischer was exceptional in the extent to which he, perhaps more than any of his contemporaries, entered into the spirit of the artistic activity and scientific research that characterized the Rome of this period. We do not know whether he decided to visit Italy entirely of his own accord when he was probably no more than sixteen years old, or whether his father urged him to go. It is, however, reasonable to assume that his travel was made possible by the Princes of Eggenberg who were his father's patrons.

When Fischer arrived in Rome about 1671, the High Roman Baroque was already coming to an end. Almost all the great architectural undertakings of the period had already been accomplished. The Late Roman Baroque was a synthetic style and the most important architect of this period, Carlo Fontana (1634–1714), tried to bring together the achievements of the three masters of the preceding period, Pietro da Cortona, Gianlorenzo Bernini, and Francesco Borromini. There is no doubt that Fischer's own constant search for synthesis had its origin in the Late Roman Baroque. It was in Rome that he came into contact with the problems of town planning that had arisen in the Late Baroque period. The pair of churches dedicated to the Virgin in the Piazza del Popolo, one on each side of the beginning of the Corso, were still being built when he was in Rome. Fischer was also confronted in Rome with the final stages of the most important achievements in the field of Late Baroque interior decoration – the ceiling paintings in the Jesuit churches of the Gesù, by Giovanni Battista Gaulli (Baciccia), and S. Ignazio, by Andrea Pozzo. Fischer, unlike Bernini, was later to make extensive use of ceiling frescoes in his own buildings and it seems that this early experience of the work of Gaulli and Pozzo was to a great extent responsible for this.

In striking contrast to his immediate predecessors, the reigning Pope, Innocent XI, was distinguished as an administrator rather than as a patron of learning and the arts. Above all, he aimed to set the papal administration and finances in order, abolish nepotism, improve the education of priests, and raise moral standards generally. Faced with the challenge of Louis XIV, he reaffirmed the authority of the papacy and later he successfully persuaded the European powers to support the Emperor against the Turks. There was, however, another important intellectual centre in Rome. Queen Christina of Sweden (1626–89) had abdicated from the throne in 1654 and become a Roman Catholic, since which time she had lived for the most part in Rome in close contact with the papal court. Her residence in the Palazzo Riario in the Via della Lungara, below the Gianicolo, in which her art collections were kept, had become a meeting-place for cardinals, writers, scholars, artists and connoisseurs. In 1674 the Queen, who because of her great intellectual gifts was known as 'Pallas Suecica' among her contemporaries, founded an academy of learning in Rome, called the Accademia Reale. For thirty years the Queen remained one of the leaders of intellectual life in Rome. The city had become a magnet for important archaeologists and antiquaries. In their writings, these men tried for the first time to make scientific and archaeological reconstructions of ancient ruins, with reference to ancient coins and literary sources. Their example led to a remarkable increase in the systematic collection of antiques and also scholarly investigations of them. The same attitude inspired the writing of histories of 'modern' buildings – e.g. Rossi's *Palazzi di Roma* and Fontana's *Templum Vaticanum*.

The young sculptor from Graz seems to have found life in Rome very difficult at first. Like so many other young artists who came to Rome at this period to continue their education or to find work, Fischer could hardly manage to survive. He was rescued from this wretched situation by pure chance – someone suggested to him that he should go to Philipp Schor, a much sought-after architect and painter at the papal court. Schor was always in need of sculptors and wax-workers who could make models according to his designs. Fischer was put to work by Schor and carried out these tasks to his employer's complete satisfaction. At the same time, he also gave himself a thorough grounding in the theory of architecture. One absolutely indispensable factor in this, especially as far as building in the classical orders was concerned, was a knowledge of Vitruvius' treatise on architecture. Architects had been discussing this work constantly since the Renaissance and had added to it their own theories about architecture. Fischer demonstrated clearly in his own book on the history of architecture and in his own buildings that he had seriously studied the theoretical works of Alberti, Vignola, Palladio, Serlio and Scamozzi. (He was also intimately acquainted with the works which Guarini and Pozzo published at this time and later.) An equally important part, however, was played in his education as an architect by his thorough study of the ancient Roman buildings still standing in the city and of the works of the great Renaissance and Baroque architects.

Philipp Schor (b. 1646) was responsible for introducing Fischer to the most outstanding artists and architects of the period and to his first patron. It was through Schor that he came into contact with the papal court, with the circle of scholars and artists gathered around Queen Christina of Sweden and with Bernini's studio. Schor himself was a member of a long-established family of artists from the Tyrol. His father, Johann Paul Schor, also known as

Giovanni Paolo Tedesco, was a well-known decorator and painter at the papal court who had worked in Cortona's studio and had taken part, together with other disciples of Cortona, in the decoration of the Palazzo Quirinale. He and his brother Egid had also carried out the decorative parts of the great ceiling fresco of the gallery of the Palazzo Colonna in Rome. Later, as a member of Bernini's studio, he worked for the papal court and specialized in festive decorations, architectural ornament, state carriages and furniture, embroidery and centre-pieces for banqueting tables. He was also responsible for the ornamentation of Bernini's *Cathedra Petri* in St Peter's. In his later years, he was assisted by his elder son Philipp who, like his father, specialized in ephemeral architecture for festive occasions. He too was a painter at the papal court but, unlike his father, practised architecture proper. The Schors lived in the Piazza di Spagna.

Through the Schors Fischer gained access to Bernini's studio and was able to study at close hand many of his unpublished and hitherto unexecuted designs and plans. We know from his own work the extent to which he was influenced by these. He may have met Philipp Schor's father, Johann Paul Schor (d. 1674), and Bernini himself. His knowledge of Bernini's studio, however, dated mainly from the period when it was in the hands of Carlo Fontana who carried on there after Bernini's death in 1680. Although Fontana's buildings as such exerted relatively little influence on Fischer, his constant preoccupation with synthesis undoubtedly had a decisive influence on Fischer's attitude towards the problems of architectural design. It is not known whether Fischer collaborated with others in Bernini's studio mainly on architectural projects or whether he was principally employed as a sculptor. What is certain, however, is that he was trained there in the art of designing and making medals. His teacher seems to have been Giovanni Francesco Travani, Bernini's leading pupil in this art. Fischer must have been very highly thought of as a medallist quite early in his career, because he was given a commission to do work for the Spanish envoy at the papal court.

As a result of his association with Bernini and his studio Fischer came into contact with the circle of scholars who were gathered around Queen Christina. A very friendly relationship, which had for long existed between the Queen and Bernini, became even closer in the last years of the artist's life, when they shared a deepening mysticism. Fischer received drawings of ancient vases from the Queen and was allowed to study her own collections. He also had access to the other great collections of antiques in Rome. Many of the drawings he made at this time were to be published later, in modified forms, in his history of architecture.

His contacts in Rome with the circle of archaeologists and antiquaries enabled him to acquire considerable knowledge of ancient
art and, what is more, of the scientific methods which were then
beginning to be used in the study of archaeology. This formed the
basis for his own attitude towards the ancient world. Later on he
was to make use of the works of these Roman archaeologists in
his own history of architecture. Among them was the scholarly
Jesuit Athanasius Kircher (1602–80), who taught at the Collegium
Romanum, was the Pope's librarian, and was also very highly
regarded by Queen Christina. It may also have been thanks to
Johann Paul Schor, who had illustrated works by Kircher, that
Fischer came to know him personally. Kircher was a highly versatile man – mathematician and physicist as well as universal
historian and archaeologist. He enjoyed considerable fame in his
lifetime as an Egyptologist – though his work in this field is not
very highly valued nowadays. He wrote many books on biblical
and Roman antiquities and on eastern Asia. He also possessed a
great collection of Egyptian works of art, which was later bequeathed to the Pope and is known as the Museo Kircheriano.
The beginnings of Fischer's interest in ancient Egyptian art and
architecture are undoubtedly to be found here.

Fischer was also personally in touch with the art theorist and
painter Pietro Bellori (c. 1615–96), who was the custodian of
Queen Christina's art collections and for a time the secretary of
the Accademia di San Luca where he also taught the theory of art
for a time. His most famous book, a collection of biographies of
seventeenth-century artists – Le vite de' pittori, scultori ed architetti
moderni (1672) – is prefaced by the address he had given to the
Academy in 1664, 'L'idea del pittore, dello scultore e dell'architetto
scelta dalle bellezze naturali superiore alla natura'. In this address,
he outlined the principles of an idealistic view of art, which formed
the theoretical introduction to his work.

One of the consequences of the union of the Academies of Paris
and of San Luca was that theories of art based on French classicism
as well as French art itself became very popular in Rome. Many
French artists came to work there. While Fischer was in Rome, the
painter Charles Lebrun was elected Principe of the Roman Academy
in 1676 and Charles Errard, who had acted as his deputy in Rome,
was made Principe in 1678. In 1681 the Roman Academy adopted
the statutes of the French Academy. There can be little doubt that
Fischer became familiar with the French theory of art as well as
with French architecture while he was in Rome. (He no doubt
gained his knowledge of French architecture by studying engravings.) He was also acquainted with Bellori himself at the time
when this many-sided artist and scholar was preparing material for

his book on the Roman triumphal arches, *Veteris Arcus August-orum* . . . , published in Rome in 1690. It was clearly from Bellori that Fischer learned the methods that he used later in his archaeological reconstructions.

While Fischer was in Rome, Philipp Schor introduced him to architecture and in particular to *Scheinarchitektur*: temporary buildings and decorations for festal and ceremonial occasions. While he was working in Bernini's studio he was trained in carving and modelling as well as in designing and making medals. Eventually he gained a deep insight into the art of the ancient world and into methods of reconstruction from the archaeologists and antiquaries whom he met in Rome. Both the relics of ancient Rome and the more recently constructed buildings in the city remained deeply impressed on his mind as great and unparalleled examples of outstanding architecture. He also made a number of drawings of ancient and modern buildings, of vases and works of sculpture.

His first commission came to him through Philipp Schor. In 1679 and 1682 he made two bronze medals of King Charles II of Spain at the request of the Spanish envoy to the papal court, Don Gaspar Guzman d'Haro, the Marchès del Carpio. These two medals reveal the extent to which Fischer was faithful to the ideas of Bernini.

The Spanish envoy was made Viceroy of Naples in 1683 and appointed Philipp Schor to be his court architect there. Fischer followed Schor to Naples – he was certainly in Naples by 1685 at the latest. The new Viceroy was very active in the city. He regulated the monetary system and ordered a mint, new fortifications, and an aqueduct to be built. He also possessed great art treasures and commissioned the Neapolitan architect Francesco Picchiatti (or Picchetti) to go throughout the length and breadth of Italy in search of objects for his collections. Fischer drew some of the vases in the Viceroy's collection of antiques and studied Picchiatti's private collection, but we do not know what else he did in Naples. We only know that he was extremely useful to Philipp Schor and that he had acquired considerable wealth by the time he decided to return to Austria.

It is difficult to say why he eventually made up his mind to leave Italy after some sixteen successful years there. A later member of the Schor family, to whom we are indebted for our knowledge of Fischer's relationships with this Tyrolean family of artists, reported that he returned home, according to Fischer's own words, because he had no confidence in an Italianized German. It is, however, not clear whether the person referred to was in fact Philipp Schor. The allusion may equally well have applied to Fischer himself, who was, after so many years in Italy, no longer a provincial sculptor from

Styria, but an architect, sculptor, medallist, theoretician of architecture and archaeologist with a universal education. He left Graz a
journeyman practising sculpture in a provincial tradition: he returned from Italy a rich man of the world. Was he aware of the fact
that his return was extremely well timed? It does rather look as
though he deliberately chose to return at that particular moment.
Almost everything that he undertook in his life was the result of a
conscious decision with a definite aim in mind.

A distinct change had taken place in Fischer's homeland while he
had been away in Italy. Austria had, in short, become a great
European power. The Emperor wanted his power as an absolute
monarch, the equal of Louis XIV, to be represented visibly in
magnificent imperial buildings; and his nobles naturally strove to
emulate him by erecting splendid palaces. The Church of the
Counter-Reformation had also gained a powerful impetus from the
defeat of the pagan Turks by the Catholic forces. In church architecture the clergy wanted to glorify this victory over the infidel as
well as that over the Reformation. The economic recovery which
followed the military victory resulted in the rapid recultivation and
rebuilding of the territories laid waste by the war. Most of the
country seats of the nobility had been destroyed by the Turks and
many of the villages had been burnt down in the eastern parts of
Lower Austria and Styria in 1683. The suburbs of Vienna had also
been severely damaged. After the danger of a Turkish assault had
ceased, a whole chain of palaces, built for the noble families, arose
in the outskirts and in the country surrounding Vienna. Even the
middle classes began to erect stately mansions. There was hardly
any space left inside the fortified city itself for further building, and
new buildings could only be erected on the sites of houses destroyed
during the siege, or else if older buildings were pulled down or
altered. As a consequence new suburbs sprang up around the city.
The other Austrian cities, especially Graz, Innsbruck and Salzburg
(which was at the time the capital of an independent principality
governed by a prince archbishop), were also extended systematically.

During the seventeenth century most of the architects working
in Vienna, and in Austria generally, were Italians who built mainly
in the north Italian Mannerist style with the addition of various
individual features of the Early Roman Baroque. There was an
almost complete absence of important indigenous architects.
Fischer's arrival was therefore very opportune. He was full of ideas,
but at the same time not too young – he was just thirty-one at the
time – and had had a good deal of practical experience. What is
more important perhaps is that he came from Rome and in particular
from Bernini's studio, was acquainted with the most significant
achievements of the High and Late Roman Baroque and brought

with him a great number of architectural plans and drawings. In other words, he was not only a modern architect but also a many-sided and well-educated artist who could undertake many different tasks. His buildings were far more modern than those of the Italians in Austria, and the Emperor and nobility soon recognized his superior qualities. It is, of course, possible that a feeling of national self-assertion, which was undeniably present at this period, played a part in this preference for an indigenous architect, but this was certainly a far less important motive than the simple fact of Fischer's evident artistic superiority.

From 1687 onwards Fischer was employed in Vienna and in Graz at the same time by the Emperor Leopold I. It is quite astonishing that he should have been given work by the Emperor himself so soon after his return from Italy. It is possible, of course, that the Princes of Eggenberg and his godfather, who was a counsellor and secretary in the local government of Styria, recommended him; and presumably he brought recommendations back with him from Italy. During these first years of his professional life in Austria, he was more concerned than later in his career with all kinds of plastic arts and even with the minor arts. He designed a votive column, made reliefs, medals, ivory carvings, even snuff boxes, and designed stucco decorations and vases. In addition, he designed gardens with ornamental gates and belvederes and eventually he began to design his first real buildings. It would seem that he accepted all kinds of commissions, almost as though he wanted to show how versatile he was. For a man who had only just come back from Italy, the number of commissions he received is certainly amazing. There is no doubt too that his first patrons, the Princes of Eggenberg, recommended him to other noble families in Austria to whom they were related – the Liechtensteins, the Althanns, the Dietrichsteins and the Schwarzenbergs.

His first task in Vienna was a design made in 1687 for the Dreifaltigkeitssäule, a column to the Holy Trinity, on the Graben. Emperor Leopold I had solemnly promised to erect it during the plague in 1679, and a wooden column had immediately been set up. Of the present stone column, which replaced it, only the pedestal with its six reliefs of biblical scenes was built according to Fischer's design. The marble reliefs clearly express his training in the art of making medals and his knowledge of the work of Donatello and Ghiberti (these reliefs were completed by another sculptor and medallist, Johann Ignaz Bendl). At the same time, Fischer designed the stucco decoration for the interior of the mausoleum of the Styrian line of the Habsburgs in Graz. In its general disposition his decoration conformed to the Mannerist architecture of the building by Pietro de Pomis (begun 1614). The stucco figures themselves, however, made by Italian stucco workers, follow the style of Roman stucco used in the Gesù and San Ignazio. The ornamentation is clearly influenced by the acanthus ornaments favoured by Johann Paul Schor. While Fischer was engaged in this task, he was also busy designing and making medals and carving ivory. He made an ivory relief as well as a medal with a portrait of Lodovico Antonio Burnacini, the architect to the imperial court with whom he collaborated in the column on the Graben in Vienna. (The column was completed in accordance with Burnacini's designs.) In another of his medals, which shows an astonishing gift for characterization, Fischer portrayed an unknown man – it might be a self-portrait. In expressive realism both these medals are far superior to those of Bernini's pupils.

In 1689 he was given convincing proof of the Emperor's confidence in him. Leopold appointed him to teach perspective and the theory and history of architecture to his elder son Joseph, who was eleven at the time. This was, of course, proof not only that Fischer himself, but also that architecture was very highly regarded. It was in fact considered to be a suitable and practical activity for the future Emperor and Fischer gave the boy, who is said to have shown considerable talent, an hour's instruction each day for several years. His pupil was to become his second royal and later imperial patron.

Prince Johann Adam Andreas von Liechtenstein was the first patron to provide Fischer with the opportunity to prove his worth as a practising architect. It was for this Prince's palace in the Viennese suburb of Roßau that Fischer designed a garden with a belvedere and park gates [1, 2, 3]. He also designed stables for the same Prince's country seat, Schloss Eisgrub in Moravia (now Lednice in Czechoslovakia), which were more of a palace for horses than simply stables. The Prince's father had been an amateur student of architecture and had left behind a manuscript, *Von der Architektur*, in which he discussed the theories of mid-seventeenth-century French architecture. Fischer was undoubtedly acquainted with the contents of this manuscript, and with seventeenth-century French architecture besides; he had become familiar with it in Italy by studying theoretical works and engravings. His stables at Eisgrub were built in accordance with the late Prince's ideas and enabled him to put his knowledge of French architecture into practice.

In 1688 Fischer was living in a sculptor's house in Vienna, which was near the church of Maria am Gestade at the 'Fischerstiege', when he became seriously ill and was cared for by Prince Anton Florian von Liechtenstein. The Prince wrote to his brother, Maximilian Jakob Moriz, that he hoped to keep a great 'virtuoso' alive. It is obvious that the noblemen for whom Fischer worked not only valued him for what he did for them, but also realized that they were employing a man of extraordinary personality.

Fischer was publicly recognized as an architect of outstanding ability when his two 'triumphal arches' were erected in Vienna. These were built to mark the entry into the city of his pupil, Joseph, on his return from coronation as King in Frankfurt am Main in the spring of 1690 [7, 8]. Fischer's success was celebrated by the 'nationalist' party at the imperial court in Vienna as a resounding victory over those who favoured the Italian artists at the court. The supporters of the 'nationalist' policy saw a future opponent of Louis XIV in the person of the young King. In 1694 the Emperor's son set up his own court and Fischer became a member of it. Besides being held in high esteem by the imperial family, he received numerous commissions from the Austrian nobility. He designed, for example, a palace in the city [41] and a hunting lodge in the country, Schloss Neuwaldegg, for the Court Chancellor, Theodor Althet Heinrich Graf Stratmann. He designed a garden palace in the suburbs of Vienna on the Danube for the Lord High Steward, Christian Johann Graf Althann [64], and another hunting lodge, to the north-east of Vienna, for the man who had commanded the troops defending the city against the Turks, Ernst Rüdiger Graf Starhemberg [50]. Prince Eugene of Savoy commissioned him to build a town palace [42, 44–6], but there must have been serious disagreements between them, because the Prince did not go back to Fischer for any of his later buildings, but turned instead to Fischer's rival, Lucas von Hildebrandt.

Fischer also had many commissions outside Vienna. The city which offered him the greatest scope for developing his gifts as a builder of churches and as a town planner was undoubtedly Salzburg. Ever since the sixteenth century, the residence of the Prince Archbishop of Salzburg had been an important centre of north Italian Mannerism beyond the Alps. Towards the end of the seventeenth century, the Italian Baroque style of architecture had begun to establish itself in Salzburg with the arrival of the architect Caspar Zugalli (or Zuccalli) from Munich. The Prince Archbishop of Salzburg, Johann Ernst Graf Thun (1687–1709), however, had an aversion to Italian artists and architects – in which respect he was similar to the 'nationalists' at the Viennese court – and dismissed them. A few years earlier Zugalli had begun to build the church of the Theatine monks, who had come from Munich and established themselves in Salzburg, but this work now came to a standstill. Unlike his predecessors, the new Archbishop did not look to north Italy or Munich for guidance in art and architecture, but to the imperial court in Vienna, appointing Johann Bernhard Fischer to be his new architectural adviser and inspector of buildings.

Archbishop Thun was the last in a long line of great princes of the Church in Salzburg, who had in common strong personalities and a deep love of the arts. Sternly religious to the verge of asceticism, he constantly sought to strengthen the Christian faith in his principality. He created a great number of religious foundations, as we shall see, and financed the building of these not only by managing his own estates and property very skilfully and by making use of the general wave of economic prosperity, but also by exploiting another source of revenue. As a young man making the 'grand tour' of Europe, he had come into contact with the Dutch East-India Company and had invested in it. This investment bore rich fruit. The company had trading stations on the islands of the Malay Archipelago and on the mainland of south-east Asia and imported spices, sugar and coffee from these territories. The produce of the company was sold twice a year in Amsterdam. One of the most charming consequences of the Archbishop's connections with the Dutch East-India Company is the famous Salzburg carillon. The bells were founded in 1688 and 1689 in the Netherlands and the Archbishop acquired them soon afterwards. It was not until between 1702 and 1704, when suitable specialists were available, that it was possible to hang them in Salzburg. (The upper part of the bell-tower may perhaps go back to an idea of Fischer's.)

The Archbishop used the revenue that he derived from trade in the most liberal manner for social and religious foundations. He founded, for example, a college for priests, with the Dreifaltigkeits-kirche in the middle [18, 20, 22, 23], and had a special church, the Kollegienkirche [24, 27–31], built for the Benedictine University of Salzburg. He also founded a hospital for pilgrims, students, priests, journeymen and poor people, the hospital of St John the Baptist [32, 34, 35], called in the sisters of the Ursuline order for the task of educating girls, and had a church built for them [37, 38]. He and other members of his family founded the Kirchenthal pilgrimage church, which is dedicated to the Virgin and located near Lofer in the Salzburg mountains [36]. Moreover, he had his residence in Salzburg splendidly fitted out [16] and a new summer residence, Schloss Klesheim [66, 67], built outside Salzburg itself. All these buildings were designed by Fischer. For these activities the architect received not only 500 florins and later 750 florins per annum, but also a considerable amount of wine from the Archbishop's estates in south Tyrol, in accordance with the custom prevalent at the time. Fischer went several times a year to Salzburg, checking the work which the provincial architects, who were in fact building contractors, were carrying out according to his designs and models.

The domes and towers of Fischer's churches changed the whole appearance of Salzburg, giving the city the skyline that delights us today. The Archbishop, whose sight was failing, probably saw them only indistinctly. But these buildings provided his last resting place, since his mortal remains were divided between the Cathedral and three of the religious foundations he had commissioned. He was buried in the Cathedral, but his heart was placed in the Church of the Holy Trinity, near the priests' college, his brain in the University Church and his bowels in the hospital church of St John the Baptist. With the death of this prelate, Fischer lost one of his most generous and understanding patrons. His successor, Franz Anton Prince Harrach, dismissed Fischer at once and replaced him with his rival, Johann Lucas von Hildebrandt. Fischer had planned to publish engravings of twelve of the buildings that had been built under Archbishop Thun, but was unable to do so.

During the last decade of the seventeenth century a considerable number of buildings were erected according to Fischer's designs in Vienna and Salzburg, as well as in Lower Austria, Moravia and Styria. He declared that he had fourteen important works in hand in 1693 alone. It was, of course, possible for him to do this only by leaving the practical task of executing his plans to others and confining himself mainly to checking the progress of the various buildings from time to time. It would seem that the only works he supervised in person were the great imperial buildings in Vienna and the high altar for the pilgrimage church of Mariazell in Styria [71], the national shrine of Austria. For a man of his times he travelled an extraordinary amount. For instance, we find him at one time in Salzburg and at another in Moravia, then a little later he is back again in Styria. In 1691 he was in Prague, studying sixteenth- and seventeenth-century buildings. He was also a man whose activities were astonishingly diverse. In 1696 he produced a plan for controlling a particularly dangerous and rocky part of the river Danube near Grein. His proposal was to make use of the unusually low water level at that time and to blow up the rocks to reduce the risk to shipping. The plan was approved by the authorities but it is not known whether or not it was carried out. It seems, however, that successful attempts to reduce the danger in this part of the river were not made until much later. (It was only with the building of the great barrage at Persenbeug after the Second World War that the danger was completely removed.)

It is a clear illustration of the range of Fischer's interests and abilities that, as well as forming engineering projects of this kind, he also made designs for applied art. Fischer's ideas can be traced in a number of liturgical vessels wrought by the court goldsmith Johann Känischbauer. The most famous of them is the monstrance of the Church of Maria Loreto in Prague, made at the bequest of one Gräfin Kolowrat and originally containing 6,138 pieces of diamond weighing $755\frac{1}{8}$ carats – the property of the deceased lady. Using motifs derived from Bernini, Fischer created a sacred vessel of quite extraordinary form, depicting the redemption of the world through the mediation of the Immaculate Virgin who overcomes all evil. The foot of the monstrance is a writhing serpent which bears the globe of the world. The Virgin stands in triumph on the world and the Host appears to float above her with its diamond-studded halo.

In 1690, soon after his great public success with the temporary triumphal arches, Fischer married Sophia Konstantia Morgner, the daughter of a notary from Ratisbon. In the first years of their marriage, the couple lived in the house of a physician in the Kärtnerstrasse in Vienna. They had five children; King Joseph I was the godfather of their first son, who died in infancy. The second son, the architect Joseph Emanuel Fischer, who was born in 1693, and two of three daughters also survived their father. As the imperial and royal architect, Fischer was raised to the nobility in 1696 and allowed to use the title of von Erlach, which was derived from the name of his mother's first husband, the sculptor Sebastian Erlacher.

Fischer was at the height of his career at the turn of the seventeenth and eighteenth centuries. It was at this time that he was building Schloss Schönbrunn for King Joseph [65]. With the Emperor's permission, he had engravings made of this palace and sent them all over Europe in order to draw attention to what he had done in the service of the Viennese court and probably also in order to gain new patrons. Two of the men to whom he sent engravings were Frederick I, who had recently been crowned King in Prussia and was well known to be a patron of art and science, and Duke Frederick II of Saxe Gotha.

The War of the Spanish Succession (1701–14) did not at first have too damaging an effect on the imperial building programme, but, as time went on, it began to make heavier and heavier demands on the Emperor's financial resources. But the war also had a favourable effect on Fischer's life. The Emperor's alliance with Prussia, Holland and England made it possible for Fischer to study the architecture of those countries. From about 1700 onwards a change can be detected in the style of his work, brought about by his increasing interest in the architecture of Palladio and his successors. Rome and Paris were at that time no longer the most important centres of architecture. These had undoubtedly become London and, rather a long way behind, the Protestant courts in northern Europe. Fischer was naturally very anxious to study this new architecture and, in 1704, Emperor Leopold I gave him a letter of recommendation to visit the court of Frederick I of Prussia. He introduced himself in Berlin with a design for a Lustschloss for the King [70], but he was not given a commission to build it. All the same, he did have an opportunity to study the works of an important colleague, Andreas Schlüter, who, like himself, was a sculptor and architect and owed a great deal to Bernini. From Berlin Fischer went, presumably via Holland, to England. He had already been in correspondence with Dutchmen and had received drawings of Dutch buildings from them. His later buildings in Vienna show that he also studied seventeenth-century English architecture. The greatest achievement of the English Baroque, St Paul's Cathedral, was being built when he was in London. It is possible too that he was finally encouraged to write his history of architecture while he was in London and perhaps by Sir Christopher Wren himself. Certainly he began to work on it as soon as he had returned home from England [105–10]. Ideas for a history of architecture, and its origins in the Temple of Solomon in Jerusalem, have been discovered in Wren's literary legacy. We may certainly assume that the two architects met in London. It was probably in England, too, that new sources for his attempts to reconstruct ancient buildings were disclosed to him. There can be little doubt that in England he encountered the same interest in archaeology and research into classical antiquity as he had found in Rome in the circle of archaeologists and antiquaries at the court of Queen Christina. The aim of Fischer's journey to Protestant northern Germany, Holland and England was to keep up to date with recent architectural developments. Soon after his return to Austria, he decided that he must study Palladianism at its source and consequently went to Venice in 1707. This cannot, of course, have been his first visit to the city, because his return journey from Rome to Graz and Vienna must have taken him through Venice. Nor was it his last visit – he went back again for a short time in 1717. He was especially interested, during this last visit, in the Valier sepulchral monument in SS. Giovanni e Paolo.

Emperor Leopold I died in 1705 and his elder son came to the throne as Emperor Joseph I. Energetic and self-confident, Joseph was more insistent than his father had been on his rights as Emperor and more conscious of himself as the Emperor of the Holy Roman Empire, as opposed to the King of France, Louis XIV. The French King's wars of conquest had aroused a strong national feeling within the Empire and the hopes of many were placed in the young Emperor. Like his father, Joseph I was well disposed towards the arts and had even greater gifts as far as music was concerned. He was, however, prevented by the War of the Spanish Succession and by the brevity of his reign from becoming what his supporters hoped he would become, a German Sun King.

Fischer, who had been Joseph's tutor when he was a boy and a
member of his court since his coronation as King, applied for and
obtained the post of chief inspector of court buildings, for which
he received 2,000 florins a year. It seems that Fischer, to promote
his application for this post, made a design for the halberds of the
imperial *Trabantengarde* (bodyguard) – weapons which were intended
to be used at the *Erbhuldigung* on 22 September 1705, when the
'states' of Vienna and Lower Austria took their oath of allegiance
to Joseph I. The design remained, however, unexecuted.

During the first ten years of the eighteenth century, Fischer built
less than he had done in the past. There are three probable reasons
for this – first, his visit to London in 1704, second, his administrative
duties as inspector of court buildings and third, the work on his
great history of architecture. His relationship with his second
imperial patron must, however, have been extremely good. He had,
after all, taught the Emperor the principles of architecture when
Joseph was a boy and later he became court engineer, the chief
inspector of all the Emperor's palaces and buildings, and the
architect whom the Emperor favoured above all others. It was
Fischer's work which accompanied and glorified the Emperor at
every important stage of his short life (1678–1711) – his coronation,
his wedding and his death [7, 8, 72, 75].

Fischer's relationship with his third imperial patron, Leopold's
second son, Charles VI (1711–40), does not appear to have been
quite as happy. Soon after Joseph died, Fischer applied for and was
granted permission to continue as chief inspector of court buildings.
But his position as the principal architect at the Viennese court was
no longer uncontested. Many members of the court, and of the
public generally, preferred to Fischer's lofty and idealistic conceptions the more pleasing and elegant architecture of Johann
Lucas von Hildebrandt who had, by this time, become his most
dangerous rival. In order to strengthen his position at court, in 1712
Fischer presented the Emperor with the manuscript of his history
of architecture, *Entwurff Einer Historischen Architectur* ('A Plan of
Civil and Historical Architecture'). But Fischer was able to gain the
Emperor's favour by his design for the Karlskirche in Vienna [85]
more than by the dedication of his book. Hoping to save the city
from an epidemic of plague, Charles VI made a vow in 1713 to build
this church. The building Fischer conceived was intended to be a
church dedicated to the Emperor's patron saint, St Charles Borromeo; in addition it was intended as a monument to its founder,
the last Habsburg King of Spain (1703–14), and the last of the
Habsburg emperors who cherished the dream of establishing a
world-wide monarchy (like his ancestor Charles V) by uniting –
after his brother's death – the crowns of Spain and the Empire.

Although he lost Spain, this last male descendant of the house of Habsburg never forgot this idea of unity. A long reign enabled Charles VI to see his imposing architectural plans completed, to put the imperial art collections into order and to enlarge them considerably. In the open competition for the church, in which Hildebrandt and Fernando Galli-Bibbiena participated, the Emperor decided in favour of Fischer, because his designs, in their imperial grandeur, reflected his own ambitions. Similarly, Fischer succeeded, even in his last years, in obtaining the commission to renew and extend the imperial residence, the Hofburg. But only the Hofstallungen (imperial stables) [98] and the Hofbibliothek (imperial library) [99–102, 104] were built according to his designs. These three great buildings of Fischer's last years were, however, completed after his death by his son Joseph Emanuel.

Fischer was famous both as a practising architect and as a theoretician and was personally in contact and in correspondence with important scientists and thinkers of his period. The German philosopher Gottfried Wilhelm Leibniz (1646–1716), who had very spirited contacts with Emperor Charles VI, Prince Eugene of Savoy and many other members of the nobility as well as with many scientists and artists in Vienna, was very anxious to found an imperial academy of science in the city. He stayed in Vienna from 1712 until 1714 and made himself personally known to all people of influence and importance. In 1713 he wrote to Charles VI, suggesting that Fischer von Erlach should be made an honorary member of the proposed academy. Fischer designed a building with rooms which could be used for apparatus and experiments and others which would serve as meeting places for the members. But after Leibniz died, the plan for founding an academy in Vienna was dropped.

Fischer also had close connections with the Swedish-born numismatist and antiquary, Carl Gustaf Heraeus, who had been the Emperor's inspector of antiquities and medals since 1712 and was very well versed in the ancient authors and in archaeological literature. Charles VI was himself interested in numismatics and had a good collection of coins, for the arrangement of which Heraeus was responsible; he had also added to it and begun to publish it. He and Leibniz were in animated correspondence with each other. Heraeus wrote the detailed descriptions of the plates in Fischer's history of architecture.

During the last years of his life, Fischer was in touch with Conrad Adolph von Albrecht, a scholar and art lover who had at one time been the Emperor's envoy to Portugal. Later, Fischer's son, Joseph Emanuel, continued this connection with von Albrecht, who composed the programmes for the decoration of the buildings and monuments erected during the reign of Charles VI.

Even in later life, Fischer still made long journeys. In 1717 he went to Venice again to study the buildings that had been put up since his visit of 1707. In 1720 he visited Prague, where he told the painter and engineer Johann Ferdinand Schor about his life in Rome as a young man.

In the meantime, Fischer's son, Joseph Emanuel (1693–1742), had grown up and become a worthy collaborator. Joseph Emanuel was Fischer's third child but the first to survive infancy. Fischer had been very far-sighted in providing for his son from the time he was born. Joseph Emanuel's godparents were the Austrian Court Chancellor, Theodor Graf Stratmann, and his wife. Fischer himself took care of his son's education, which was extremely comprehensive, including instruction in architecture, drawing, mathematics and physics, and the study of antiquities. He was also sent to the most important centres of architecture and mathematical sciences in Europe. By the time he was seventeen years old, his skill at drawing was so far advanced that he was able to give his father's patrons, who were to be his own patrons in the future, examples of his work. He drew his father's designs and collaborated with him in his history of architecture. The older Fischer at the same time encouraged him to prepare his own collection of engravings and this was given to the master of the Emperor's horses, Philipp Sigismund Graf Dietrichstein, on his birthday in 1713. In 1715 it was published in Joseph Emanuel's name, with a foreword by Carl Gustaf Heraeus, as *Prospekte und Abriße einiger Gebäude von Wien* ('Views of Some Viennese Buildings'). It forms the counterpart or sequel to the older Fischer's history of architecture, but is almost entirely devoted to contemporary architecture and deals with the architectural revival of Vienna after the Turkish siege [47, 76].

The father prepared a great educational journey for his son, with the aim of enabling him to spend several years, as he himself had done, at foreign centres of art and learning, studying architecture in particular. In a letter written in 1713 Leibniz had told the Emperor how capable the young Fischer was, and indeed, the young man received from Charles VI a travelling scholarship of 800 florins a year for an indefinite period. At the same time, however, the Emperor commissioned him to purchase medals for the imperial collection of coins. Joseph Emanuel was in Rome from 1714 to 1715 and, like his father before him, he studied archaeology there and established contacts with famous archaeologists, including Francesco di Ficoroni. Like his father too, he probably went to Naples, which had become Austrian after the War of the Spanish Succession. After spending a short time in Vienna, probably supervising the printing of his book of engravings, Joseph

Emanuel seems to have travelled to Leiden. He then went on to Paris, where he stayed from 1717 until 1719. While he was there he was in close touch with scholars, including the antiquary Bernard de Montfaucon, and it is clear that French architecture of the period, particularly that of Robert de Cotte, made a deep impression on him. He revised many of his own designs in the light of what he had seen in Paris. He must also have visited London and have developed his mathematical and technical skills more fully there, as he did in Leiden.

In the summer of 1722 the younger Fischer went to Vienna, where he practised engineering and architecture. Just before this date, he had built a steam engine for the reigning Landgrave of Hesse-Kassel, which was modelled on those he had probably seen in England and which he set up in Kassel. In 1723 he did exactly the same in Vienna and caused a great sensation in the city. The Prince of Schwarzenberg used this engine to keep the water circulating in his garden and to make the fountains play.

The young man's educational journey, which had been subsidized by the court, came to an end in 1722; immediately on his return to Vienna, he applied for the position of architect to the court. He made it clear that he would be able to finish the buildings which his father was scarcely able to finish himself because of his advanced age and poor health. Towards the end of the year he was appointed court architect, with an annual salary of 1,500 florins. This was the beginning of a brilliant career at the imperial court. After having represented his father unofficially since his return to Vienna in 1722, he was now placed officially in charge of the building of the Karlskirche and the imperial stables, which his father had designed but had been unable to complete. In the following year, he began the work of building the imperial library in accordance with his father's plans. He made certain minor alterations to his father's designs in all three buildings. The extent of these alterations, however, is not yet sufficiently clear.

After the death of his first wife, the elder Fischer had married the widow of a lieutenant, Franziska Sophia Willer, in 1705, but she left him in old age. His two daughters seem, however, to have looked after him and his son. Financially, he was without anxiety. Apart from his yearly income of 2,000 florins, he received 650 florins each year as a reimbursement for the use of his coach and horses on the many journeys that he had to make as inspector of court buildings. In addition, he had, in his official capacity, the use of an apartment in one of the houses in the city and, in his private capacity, he owned three houses with gardens in the Wieden, a suburb of Vienna. He also enjoyed the privilege that no soldiers could be billeted in any of these houses.

In his will he disinherited his unfaithful wife, whose whereabouts were unknown to him, and bequeathed money for the foundation of almshouses instead. He left his property and art collections to his son, and his capital and silver were divided equally between his daughters. After a long illness, he died on 5 April 1723 in his apartment in the Sternhof, near the old town hall in Vienna. A solemn funeral took place on the following day in the catacombs of St Stephen's Cathedral.

Although we know so much about the life and work of Fischer the architect, the sources tell us very little about him as a man. Only a few letters written in his own hand have been preserved and these deal mostly with business matters. His will contains some bitter remarks about his faithless second wife. One of his contemporaries said of him that he was a friendly man and another declared that, although he had no equals in the country, he clearly had a bee in his bonnet. But surely the same can be said about almost every great artist. In the manner of the times, he is portrayed on canvas as a knight in a characteristic pose. But portraits of him emphasize his status as a court architect raised to the nobility rather than his personality.

We shall be able to learn more about Fischer himself if we examine his works closely and try to reconstruct their original state and setting in the context of the special functions for which they were intended, also bearing in mind the social and political circumstances which determined their creation. By examining how he solved the various tasks he was given and how he – within his social and historical environment – treated architectural problems in theory and practice, we shall be able to understand the basic principles of his art and his way of thinking. In other words, a study of Fischer's works will reveal his personality.

·2·
Fischer's Works

a. The Birth of the Austrian Baroque

After his return from Italy to Vienna, Fischer did no less than create the Austrian Baroque. He created this new style by blending together the styles of the High Roman Baroque and of French architecture of the middle and late seventeenth century and by including in this synthesis many features of Italian Mannerism, which had already become traditional in Austria. But he went further beyond these architectural styles, all of which can be traced back to the Italian Renaissance, to their common source, the architecture of antiquity. He synthesized these different elements, always with ancient Rome in mind, so that the resulting work had classical dimensions. In his history of architecture he described his own works, with evident pride, as 'neo-Roman'.

At that time there was nothing discreditable in looking back to the great achievements of the past. It was, on the contrary, an honourable practice for the artist or architect of the seventeenth century, ennobling his work and enhancing its status. Only later, under the influence of the Romantic notion of creative genius, was this attitude towards art and architecture deprecated as eclecticism. Fischer himself was in no way eclectic. He regarded the great buildings of the past as raw material from which he could fashion new and quite distinctive architectural structures of his own. A careful study of Fischer's works will reveal the laws inherent in this process. In solving the various tasks with which he was confronted, he developed his own style. To be perfect, his complex architectural conceptions demanded the appropriate sculptural and painted decoration; in this way he inaugurated with his architecture the glorious period of the Austrian Baroque, which is still evident in the towns and countryside of Austria today.

Significantly enough, Fischer began his activity as an architect in Austria with a belvedere. Later in his career, too, he was to express some of his most distinctive and original ideas in the field of garden architecture, where he could give the freest possible scope to his imagination. One of the first noblemen to have a

38

garden laid out in the suburbs of Vienna after the Turkish siege of the city was Prince Johann Adam Andreas von Liechtenstein. In 1687 Fischer designed for this Prince a French park closed off with a belvedere [1] in the suburb of Roßau, outside the city walls.

Slight, rather insubstantial buildings of this kind, usually comprising open arcades and providing a fine view of the surrounding country or of the park or garden, had been known since the fifteenth century in Italy, either as independent buildings or as parts of a larger structure. Like most other independent belvederes, Fischer's building was set at the top of a slight incline. It had three main functions. In the first place, it served to close the garden off from the surrounding countryside. In the second place, it subordinated the surrounding countryside itself, which was visible in the great arch of the gate, to the dominant architectonic order of the garden. Finally, it was a vantage-point with an excellent view.

1. Belvedere for the Prince of Liechtenstein

In this belvedere Fischer succeeded in combining ancient Roman elements, the triumphal arch and the exedra, with High Baroque motifs – the symmetrically curved outside flight of stairs – in a 'spatial gate'. The whole structure was covered by a kind of dome with a central opening and flanked with wings mounted on high pedestals. The lofty 'diadem arch' resting on columns; the sharply articulated projections of the wings; the elegant curves of the outline of the roof, enlivened by decorative sculpture which accentuated the vertical elements of the structure: these elements formed, together with the concave flight of stairs and the oval basin in front of it, a façade which closed off the garden like stage scenery. Transfigured by the sparkling drops of water from the fountain, the hilly landscape outside the garden was also contained in this 'picture'.

With the conception of this very important early work Fischer had created one of his fundamental architectural motifs, known as the *Raumtor mit Flügeln*, literally the 'spatial gate with lateral wings'; I shall refer to this henceforth as the Liechtenstein belvedere motif. He varied this motif in many ways, using it as a belvedere, as a park gate, as a triumphal arch and as an altar [1–3, 8, 72, 74]. In all

2. Park gate

3. Design for park gate

its many variations, it has a strangely fascinating effect on the spectator – he becomes conscious of a blurring of the line which separates illusion from reality. I call this motif a 'spatial gate' because, on the one hand, it is possible to stand inside it and feel as secure as if one were in a room, and because, on the other hand, one can walk through it as one walks through a gate. In the Liechtenstein garden, it closed the park off from the countryside surrounding it and at the same time opened the view from the garden to the world outside. There were many French and Italian examples which might have given Fischer an initial stimulus for this invention, but there is none which can be unequivocally regarded as the direct inspiration for his belvedere in the Liechtenstein garden. This invention is typical of his extremely sculptural approach to architecture. He shows himself to be an authentic pupil of Bernini, especially in the delight that he clearly takes in the play of contrasting convex and concave forms.

The park gates [2, 3], doubtless designed by Fischer in connection with the Liechtenstein garden, were inspired by Bernini, too – probably by his façade of S. Andrea al Quirinale in Rome or by his first project for the east façade of the Louvre [55]. But Fischer completely transformed Bernini's conceptions in his idea of a 'spatial gate' with multiple functions. These park gates were apparently never built and Fischer's conception of the belvedere was only carried out in a slightly altered form. The Italian architect Domenico Martinelli, who built the belvedere, clearly did not understand the need for the arch to be slight and insubstantial in character, appearing to float above the outside flight of stairs and the basin in front of it, with the result that he changed Fischer's original plan. Canaletto painted two pictures of the Liechtenstein garden, showing the belvedere in the form in which it was built; these are now in the gallery of the Prince of Liechtenstein in Vienna. The belvedere was pulled down in 1873 to make way for a building which housed the Prince's collection of paintings.

Fischer's designs for this belvedere and for one of the park gates of the Liechtenstein garden are contained in the fifth book of his history of architecture, which is a kind of pattern book mainly composed of designs for vases. Fischer designed a great number of vases for parks [15], with decorations which either alluded to the forces of nature working in the garden or glorified the owner of the garden as one of the gods, in the manner that had become customary since the Renaissance. Some of the vases made according to Fischer's designs have been preserved in various gardens in Vienna, Lower Austria and Salzburg. The sun vase with a relief of Apollo on his chariot [1, right], for example, can be found in the park of Schloss Greillenstein in Lower Austria.

To some extent, these vases form a bizarre counterpart to the restrained and harmonious lines of his buildings. In form, they are halfway between architecture, the proportions of which are determined by the Orders, and surrounding nature. We have really to imagine these vases in a park designed in the French style, standing on monumental pedestals joined by balustrades, bordering the formal parterres with their decorative 'embroideries' of flowers and little paths of coloured sand, standing out in sharp relief against the green of the closely clipped trees, and reflected in the water of the fountains.

Fischer's models for these vases, with their dynamic outlines and the picturesque effect of light and shadow interchanging on their surfaces, were ancient vases as well as those of the Mannerist and Baroque periods, especially the ones engraved by Polidoro da Caravaggio and Jean Le Pautre. He conceived them to form a striking contrast with his buildings. The use that he later made of them in his history of architecture is proof that this was done quite consciously. Here they have the effect of *repoussoirs*, framing the buildings in the background, the harmony of the whole being made up of contrasts – a typical feature of Baroque art. The fact that Fischer devoted the whole of the fifth book of his history of architecture to vases indicates the importance with which he regarded them [1, 2, 57].

Fischer's designs for the Liechtenstein garden and for vases reveal a fundamental aspect of his attitude towards architecture – his intention of conceiving his buildings as embedded in nature. This principle had a decisive influence on Austrian Baroque architecture and continued to be one of its striking features. Significantly, one of Fischer's works was the first of a long series of Baroque buildings on hills and mountains which give such a distinctive appearance to the landscape of Austria even today.

Since 1680 Johann Michael Graf Althann had owned the estate of Frain on the river Thaya in Moravia (now Vranov nad Dyjí in Czechoslovakia). The medieval castle, which was built above the river on a hill about 250 feet high, had been severely damaged both in the Thirty Years' War and later by fire. In 1688 Fischer submitted plans, probably for the complete rebuilding of the property as a dwelling for the family rather than as a fortified castle. The first part of the new building to be constructed in accordance with Fischer's designs was the great hall above the precipice. This ancestral hall [4], which replaced the original chapel, was completed in 1695. It was basically oval in shape, eighty-five feet long and surmounted by a great dome which was not placed on a drum. This was Fischer's first practical application of one of his most cherished ideas – the oval-shaped main space which makes its full

4. Schloss Frain, Vranov, interior of ancestral hall

impression in the direction of its longitudinal axis. At Frain the
main oval space is contrasted with an oval-shaped vestibule, the
longitudinal axis of which is set at right angles to that of the
ancestral hall. The interior of the latter is articulated by ten deep
niches containing windows or doors. Above each of these niches

is an oval dormer window, its clear lines cutting deeply into the mass of the dome. These ten dormer windows, which are interconnected by galleries in the wall, constitute the only architectonic articulation of the dome itself. Each of the wall piers between the windows and the doors below the dome is framed by two pilasters on a high pedestal and between these are ten smaller niches containing statues of the owner of the palace and his ancestors.

The cavernous effect made by this large oval space and its niches can only be compared with the nymphaea built in imperial Rome and, in particular, with the ruins of the so-called Temple of Minerva Medica [5]. Since the time of the Renaissance architectural

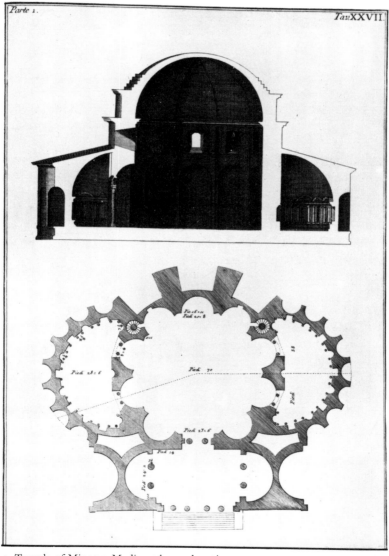

5. Temple of Minerva Medica, plan and section

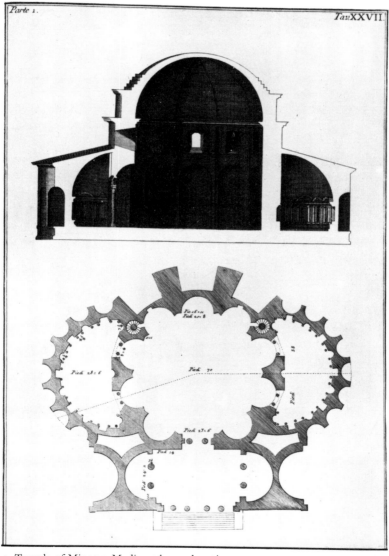

theorists had been interested in these buildings, which had, of course, a religious function. The ancestral hall of Schloss Frain should also be regarded as a kind of 'sacred' monument. This very quality is clearly revealed by the programme of its pictorial and sculptural decorations, which play such an important part in organizing the surface of its interior. In this hall, architecture, sculpture and painting unite to express one single purpose – the glorification of the Althann family. The most outstanding members of the family are immortalized in portrait statues, with their heraldic devices or mottoes inscribed and their personal actions depicted on the wall above. The characters and achievements of the individual members of the Althann family are further raised to the level of universal significance by the allegorical representation of their virtues in the lower part of the dome beside the dormer windows. At an even higher level, in the upper part of the dome, the ultimate meaning of these noble virtues is represented in an illusionistic fresco showing heaven opening, with the creative spirit and genius of the Althann family appearing as Apollo on his sun chariot, surrounded by the symbols of power, peace and plenty – in other words, the symbols of a happy and successful reign – while Fama proclaims the renown of the Althann family to the four corners of the earth. The same idea is also expressed quite clearly in the basic form of the architecture itself – the massive piers containing the statues in their niches personify the most illustrious representatives of the family, on whom the fame of the house, glorified in the dome, rests.

Architecture and the figurative arts are united here according to a homogeneous programme, the result being a *Gesamtkunstwerk* – a combination of the arts which was of a kind and consistency that had not emerged in Austria and south Germany since the Middle Ages. Architecture provided the basis upon which painting and sculpture could unfold. The figurative arts were employed not only to enhance the architectonic effect of the structure, but also to explain its significance.

Like the interior, the outside of the ancestral hall [6] was based on the ancient idea of the Roman 'mole', a massive centrally planned structure deriving its imposing effect from the fundamental simplicity of its form; the exterior of the ancestral hall is thus almost without decoration. Originally, it was closed off simply by an attic storey crowned with vases; the high pitched roof and the lateral arches are later additions. This monument to fame was consciously designed with the surrounding countryside in mind. It would seem as though Fischer's aim, in building a 'mole' on a high cliff overlooking the river valley below and dominating the entire landscape, was to perfect nature and give it a new meaning.

6. Schloss Frain, Vranov, view from river bank

It was, however, in Vienna, and with structures of an ephemeral kind, that Fischer first won public recognition. In 1690 the Emperor and Empress returned to Vienna with their twelve-year-old son, who had just been crowned King in Frankfurt am Main. The imperial family travelled down the Danube and entered the city in solemn procession, first going along the street known as the Wollzeile, where the wool merchants lived. Here, the foreign merchants, who enjoyed the special privilege of being able to set up trading stations in Vienna, had had a triumphal arch erected [7]. Then the procession passed the Cathedral of St Stephen, near which, at the Stock im Eisen, the Vienna city council had had built a second triumphal arch [8]. A third arch stood in front of the entrance to the Imperial Palace – the Hofburg – on the Kohlmarkt. Fischer was responsible for the design of the first two arches, both of which were enthusiastically praised by his contemporaries.

Since the late Middle Ages temporary buildings had often been erected in cities to mark the state entry of a ruling sovereign, and later came to play an important part in court ceremonial. They also became a source of interest to architectural theorists, especially after the idea of adapting the Roman triumphal arch for such occasions was revived in Renaissance Italy. Fischer became acquainted with this type of temporary architecture in Bernini's studio, and particularly through Johann Paul Schor and his son Philipp, who were both famous for their festive decorations at the papal court. It may be assumed that Fischer was inspired by this Roman High Baroque festival architecture, though very few illustrations of such temporary buildings survive and Fischer's own works of this kind differ essentially from them. Fischer selected several independent motifs from ancient Roman triumphal architecture and combined them in such a way that they looked like a unified whole to the spectator. His festival buildings, moreover, did not merely provide a background for pageantry but were three-dimensional structures which presented a succession of constantly changing forms to those who moved around or through them. The idea of bringing independent structural elements together in this way derives from seventeenth-century France – François Blondel, for example, had put it into practice in his designs for the Porte Saint-Denis in Paris (1672) and, only a few years before Fischer's arches were erected, had discussed its theory in his Cours d'architecture (Paris, 1683, 4e partie, liv. 12, chap. vi, p. 618 ff.).

In the arch of the foreign merchants [7] Fischer combined three elements – the triumphal arch, the triumphal column, and the statue of the ruler enthroned on the globe. For the triumphal arch he used the motif he had employed for the Liechtenstein belvedere. Like the 'diadem arch' of the belvedere [1], it rested on columns

LEOPOLDO MAGNO, ELEONORÆ AUGUSTÆ, IOSEPHO GLORIOSO
Arcum hunc Triumphalem Negotiatores Privilegiati Extranei posverunt
Viennæ MDCXC

7. Triumphal arch of the foreign merchants, 1690

D. Joannes Bernardus Fischer invenit & delineavit. Emblemata verò R.R. Dominus Carolus Josephus de la Bussie Canonicus Viennensis.

8. Triumphal arch of the city council, 1690

and had a round opening in the middle. The triumphal columns
with spiral reliefs were another of Fischer's favourite motifs. He
seemed to defy all normal laws of gravity by placing them over
the lateral passages of the triumphal arch. They and the globe seem
to float above the arch itself. The arch of the city council [8] was a
two-storeyed triumphal gate. Its lower part was a combination of
a circular temple and a triumphal arch with the main opening
capped, in the manner of Borromini, by Fischer's favourite 'diadem
arch'. Above this structure he placed a second, but lighter and less
substantial, triumphal gate, the form of which was in striking
contrast to that below. This served as the framework for the
quadriga of the triumphal monarch.

Both these structures were richly decorated with sculpture. The
statues, emblems and trophies contrasted strongly with the relatively simple forms of the architecture itself. It was chiefly the use
of dynamic sculpture which perfected the harmonious effect of
these triumphal arches in silhouette. They must be imagined with
their surfaces marbled, painted, and partly gilded. Like the ancestral
hall at Frain, each was a *Gesamtkunstwerk* glorifying the young
King Joseph, the Emperor and the Empress. The decorations for
both gates were, in fact, based on iconographical programmes
drawn up by a Canon of the Cathedral chapter in Vienna. Fischer
was especially talented in realizing such allegorical conceptions by
the ingenious combination of architectural and sculptural motifs,
each conveying a particular meaning.

The arch of the foreign merchants [7] was a glorification of the
reign of Emperor Leopold I and his consort – they were depicted
enthroned on the globe, which was in turn supported by personifications of the four quarters of the earth. The Emperor's victory
over the Turks was symbolized by statues of captive enemies, by
bundles of trophies and by reliefs on the columns depicting cavalry
battles. Leopold's victory was thought to be based on his religious
faith and on his virtues as a ruler – the allegorical personifications
of these supported and crowned the triumphal columns. The
Emperor had fought bravely against all dangers – like Hercules
and Samson, whose statues stood above the central gateway. As a
consequence of his victory, the country was prosperous and over-
flowing – this was symbolized by the statues of river gods pouring
water out of urns. Finally, a brilliant future was in sight – the young
King Joseph was represented as Apollo on a throne of clouds,
holding the sceptre in his right hand, rising like the sun and illumi-
nating the world with his rays. His glory was proclaimed by the
trumpets of Fame.

The much larger arch of the city council [8] symbolized the
triumph of Joseph I as the glorification of the house of Habsburg.

Allegories of Fame held the crown of the Holy Roman Empire over his chariot, under which his emblem with the motto *amore et timore* shone and around which were gathered personifications of the Habsburg patrimonial dominions. On the upper part of the arch, Emperor Leopold and his consort were shown accepting the homage of the cities which had been liberated from the Turks. The lower part of the arch contained statues of their ancestors and various emblems pointed to the merits and achievements of the latter as statesmen and military leaders. The very person of the young Sun King Joseph I who was glorified here seemed to prefigure the dynasty's happy future.

The enormous effect made by these two examples of ephemeral architecture was due to the fact that nothing like them had ever been seen in Vienna before. The third arch built – not by Fischer – to mark the conclusion and climax of the imperial family's triumphal entry into Vienna in 1690 was, relatively speaking, a failure. It was a ponderous four-sided (quadrifrontine) archway and looked like a piece of painted stage scenery. Fischer's two arches, on the other hand, were richly articulated three-dimensional structures, consisting of many different architectural motifs. Both of his arches were composed of elements derived from several sources – antiquity, the Roman Baroque, and the most recent French architecture. From whatever point of view they were seen, each presented a well-integrated and picturesque appearance. Fischer was lionized, and the young King's tutor in political science and history, Wagner von Wagenfels, celebrated Fischer's triumphal arches in his book glorifying the Holy Roman Empire, *Ehren-Ruff Teutschlands, Der Teutschen Und Ihres Reichs*, as the beginning of a truly German art. Wagner was the main theoretical exponent of that political party at court which believed that the idea of the Empire should be stressed in opposition to France and which tried to make the young Joseph I a second Sun King.

This was the political climate in which Fischer's greatest architectural project was evolved – the first design for Schloss Schönbrunn [9]. It was, of course, an ideal plan for a building of enormous dimensions and quite impossible to execute in view of the limited financial resources of the Viennese court at the time. The plan was published later in Fischer's history of architecture; the accompanying text reveals clearly enough the architect's disappointment at having had to abandon his plan for building such a magnificent palace on the hill of Schönbrunn and at having had to construct instead a much smaller hunting lodge in the valley below [65]. The latter was begun for the young King Joseph I in 1696. But it is not known when Fischer designed his first project or even for whom it was intended. On the death of his mother in 1686, Emperor

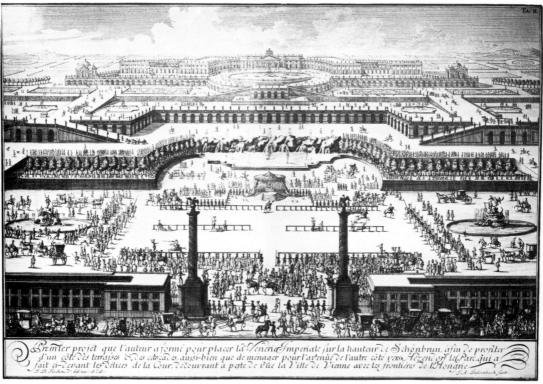

Premier projet que l'auteur a formé pour placer la Venerie Imperiale sur la hauteur de Schönbrun, afin de profiter d'un côté des terrasses & des cascades, aussi-bien que de menager pour l'avenüe de l'autre côté vers Hezendorff le Parc, qui a fait ci-devant les délices de la Cour, découvrant à perte de vûe la Ville de Vienne avec les frontieres de l'Hongrie.
I. B. Fischer D. Architect. del.   *I. A. Delsenbach fecit.*

9. First project for Schloss Schönbrunn

Leopold I became the owner of the hunting lodge Katterburg,
which was situated on the river Wien near the village of Hietzing,
outside Vienna. From 1693 onwards documents refer to the forth-
coming building of a new palace; in the meantime Fischer must
have produced his first project for a palace situated on the hill.
Fischer himself described this first project as a 'Venerie Imperiale',
an imperial hunting lodge, in the first edition of his history of
architecture, published in 1721. By then, however, the Emperor
Joseph I had been dead for ten years and Schönbrunn Palace, as
built by Fischer, had become the residence of the Empress Dow-
ager. In 1721 nobody would have spoken of Joseph I as King
('römischer König'), though that had been his title when Fischer
began to construct the palace. Yet it has been assumed that Fischer
produced his first project as early as 1688, and that he intended it
not so much as a practical scheme as simply in order to attract the
attention of Leopold I; and further, that this led to his appointment as tutor in architecture to the Emperor's elder son, Joseph.
Consequently the project has been considered as a kind of credential
which Fischer presented to the Emperor to provide evidence of
his abilities as an architect. Although there is a great deal to be said

in favour of this hypothesis, the arguments, insofar as they are based on historical fact, are not entirely convincing. The name 'Venerie Imperiale', or Emperor's hunting lodge, in the engraving of 1721 need not necessarily apply to the Emperor Leopold I. Nor can the fact that at the end of September 1690 Fischer signed a contract to erect a fountain in Brno, the capital of Moravia, and that this work, completed in 1696, bears a very close resemblance to the left-hand fountain in his first Schönbrunn project, be regarded as conclusive proof that the latter was designed some time before 1690. (At the beginning of 1690 Joseph was crowned King.) On the other hand, the chariot of Apollo above the central part of the palace in the first Schönbrunn project is identical with the chariot on the triumphal arch of the city council of 1690 [8], which undoubtedly glorifies Joseph.

In any case, Fischer conceived Schönbrunn Palace as the residence of the ruler of the Holy Roman Empire. Perhaps he intended it for the present as well as the future ruler – after all, his triumphal arches, too, glorified both father and son and thus the continuation of the dynasty. From this residence the ruler would have been able to view the capital city of his Empire and even see as far as Hungary, the crown of which he also wore. It was to be a palace worthy of the magnificence of the ruler of the Holy Roman Empire, a palace which would leave all the other palaces that had ever been built, including Versailles, in the shade. In Fischer's plan the monumental entrance was situated in the valley below and framed by two triumphal columns crowned with the imperial eagle perching on the globe of the world. It consisted in the first place of a great court, or rather tilt-yard, with the ruler's throne beneath an ornate canopy. The statues on both sides of the triumphal columns and the left-hand fountain glorified him as a second Hercules and the right-hand fountain depicted him as the sun god Apollo. The fountain on the left also symbolized the victory of the Roman Empire over the other three ancient Empires (Babylonian, Persian and Alexandrian). Behind this spacious courtyard the hill was to be cut into terraces, and a complicated system of wide ramps, cascades, terraces with basins and French parterres was to lead up to the huge palace itself. This configuration would have allowed sufficient space for ceremonial entries, providing a constantly changing background for the procession of carriages. The park, designed in the French style and stretching from the southern slope of the hill of Schönbrunn as far as the horizon, was to be laid out behind the palace. It would have been bounded in the west by the hills of the Wienerwald.

Fischer's ultimate model for this terraced approach to the entrance of Schönbrunn Palace may have been the Temple of

Fortuna at Praeneste (Palestrina) near Rome, which he could have known from sixteenth- or seventeenth-century reconstructions, or even from studying the ruins himself. This temple had certainly had a great influence on architects ever since the sixteenth century. The whole arrangement, with several different architectonically fashioned terraces, fountains and cascades descending from the palace to the entrance gate, is in accordance with the Italian Mannerist style of garden layout which had also become widespread in France. (An example of this is Saint-Germain-en-Laye near Paris, 1605 onwards.) The terraces supported by arcades are reminiscent of the orangery at Versailles. Fischer may have derived the idea of using two Trajan's columns at the entrance to Schönbrunn from

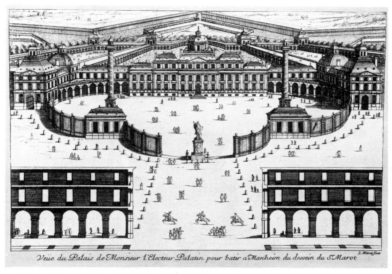

Veüe du Palais de Monsieur l'Electeur Palatin pour batir a Mannheim du dessein du S.ᵗMarot

10. Jean Marot, design for Mannheim Palace

Jean Marot's design for Mannheim Palace [10] – though it would seem more likely that he used them mainly because of their iconographical significance (the 'pillars of Hercules').

The entire width of the top terrace is taken up by the palace itself [11], which Fischer consciously designed as a kind of 'super Versailles'. He took the three *cours d'honneur* from Louis Le Vau's conception of Versailles (1668) and the idea of the central part, projecting into the park between extended lateral wings, from the later rebuilding (1678–89) by Jules-Hardouin Mansart [12]. On the entrance façade the central part of Fischer's projected palace is concave, embracing an oval basin. This device is reminiscent of Bernini's second project for the east façade of the Louvre (1665) [13]. The pedimented bay in the middle, crowned by the chariot of the monarch represented as the sun god Apollo, is recognizably

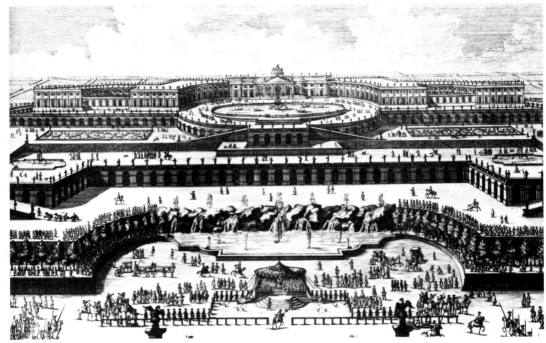

11. First project for Schloss Schönbrunn (detail)

12. Jules-Hardouin Mansart, Versailles, garden façade

similar to Carlo Maderna's façade of St Peter's and thus has an
almost religious significance. Besides 'quoting' important Roman
and French buildings in his Schönbrunn project, Fischer also
wished to represent the third important trend in the architecture
of his time, the tradition of Palladio. At each corner of the upper
terrace he placed a casino – an idea that reminds one of Vignola's
Villa Lante at Bagnaia. In their regular ground-plan – a cube with
porches on all four sides, surmounted by a dome – these casinos
are strongly reminiscent of Palladio's Villa Valmarana – La
Rotonda – at Vicenza.

13. Bernini, second project for Louvre east façade

Veue et perspective du Chasteau de Versaille du costé de la fontaine de Latone

14. Louis Le Vau, Versailles, garden façade

In the subordinate parts of the palace project as well as in detail
Fischer was once again indebted both to French architecture and
to the Palladian tradition. For example, the wing façades reflect
the style of Le Vau's garden façade at Versailles (1668) [14]. The
long ranges of open arcades and the great number of statues
adorning them are clearly influenced by north Italian villas. To

some extent Fischer also followed French architecture of his own period in, for instance, the completely undecorated utility buildings flanking the entrance, which almost resemble the 'Neue Sachlichkeit' architecture of the early twentieth century.

The first Schönbrunn project was the most important of Fischer's palace designs and the one which manifested his intentions most clearly. Once again, the chief architectural consideration was to design a residence for the ruler of the Holy Roman Empire which would surpass all the palaces that had hitherto been built by combining and harmonizing all the features used in them. Fischer's wide knowledge of the history of architecture equipped him very well indeed for this purpose. What is astonishing is the consistency with which he proceeded. His design for the palace on the hill was a combination of the most important seventeenth-century palaces – Bernini's design for the Louvre and Le Vau's and Mansart's for Versailles – decorated with Venetian villas which served as belvederes. The centre of the palace was given an almost religious significance because of its similarity with the façade of St Peter's surmounted by the figure of the ruler in the guise of the sun god in his triumphal chariot. Fischer's project also combined the two types of garden layout prevalent at the time – in front, the Mannerist terraced garden with its fountains and cascades, grottoes and lawns and, behind, on the south side, a classical French park. In this way he succeeded in transforming the landscape into a monument to the power of the Holy Roman Empire.

The most remarkable aspect of this project for Schönbrunn Palace and its gardens is that they contained nothing inhuman or disproportionate, and that Fischer managed, in his astonishing design, to find a monumental and architectonically convincing solution to the problem that confronted him. He proved that he was capable of formally subduing the most heterogeneous elements drawn from the most varied architectural styles, and of harmonizing them so fully in his design that, had it been executed, the palace would have had no equal in its period. His was undoubtedly the most idealistic of all seventeenth-century palace projects. It is hardly surprising that it proved impossible to carry it out.

We are accustomed to making distinctions between an artist's or an architect's youthful works, his mature works, and his late works. This method is not very helpful in Fischer's case. With the exception of the medals that originated in Rome and the reliefs in Vienna and Graz, we have none of his early works. (It is possible that some may eventually be found in Italy.) The buildings that he designed in Vienna and Moravia in the years immediately following his return home are mature examples of his art. By that time he was no longer looking for solutions – he had already found his style. What is more, he did not repeat himself – each of his works had its own individuality. Finally, all the architectonic motifs he was to favour throughout the rest of his life are already to be found in these works. An example of this is the emblem showing a church building on the pedestal of the right-hand column of the foreign merchants' triumphal arch of 1690 [7]. This already contains the idea of his main work, the Karlskirche, in a nutshell.

Fischer's artistic creations were more than simply individual works produced by an architect of outstanding talent. They represented for Austria the emergence of a completely new architectural style, which had an immediate effect on the work of other architects and at the same time acted as fertile soil from which new painting and sculpture grew. In this sense, the critics of 1690 were right when they declared that a new period in the history of art had been opened with Fischer's triumphal gates.

b. Church Architecture and Town Planning in Salzburg

Fischer's abilities as a town planner were fully employed in Salzburg, where almost all his projects were realized; they still dominate the pattern of the city. He probably took up his duties very soon

15. Schloss Mirabell, Salzburg, vase in park

16. Hofmarstall (archiepiscopal stables), Salzburg, façade

17 (*opposite*). Borromini, Collegio di Propaganda Fide, Rome

after the Prince Archbishop Johann Ernst Graf Thun's appointment to office in 1687. As early as 1689–90 the park of the Archbishop's summer residence, Schloss Mirabell, was redesigned according to Fischer's plans. All that is left of this work are the original entrance to the park – the visitor goes in through two pairs of symmetrically arranged gladiator statues, whose bodies to some extent form a gateway – and a few vases, the designs for which Fischer later published in his history of architecture [15].

His next task was to rebuild the Archbishop's stables. These stables, the Hofmarstall, were a complex of buildings situated at the foot of the hill called the Mönchsberg (the two festival halls, the Grosses and the Kleines Festspielhaus, are now installed in them). The summer riding school known as the Felsenreitschule was erected at the eastern end of the stables between 1690 and 1693.

By cutting three superimposed arcades out of the rock, Fischer transformed what was once a quarry in the Mönchsberg into an open-air theatre of stone. He had always been especially attracted by the striking forms produced by nature and by man's trans-formation of nature into works of art. This fascination is clearly reflected in his history of art. Fischer radically changed the west front of the existing stables, which had been built in 1607 and extended in 1662. This had been rather a sober, utilitarian build-ing, but in 1693–4 Fischer gave it a palatial façade and completely refashioned the square occupying the space between this façade, the wall of the cliff, and the hospital on the opposite side, the Bürgerspital. (The tunnel through the Mönchsberg which now connects the centre of Salzburg with its outer districts was not cut until 1764.) Fischer fitted a monumental portal into the façade of the stables and, by linking this with a richly ornamental blind win-dow above it, formed a kind of triumphal arch [16]. Many of the features of this portal are reminiscent of Borromini, especially the elegant curves of the pedestals and the cornices [17]. Fischer's main theme was the 'diadem arch', with a round opening at its vertex. The forward curve of the arch is emphasized by the vase, which appears to float above it. Despite the unmistakable echoes of Rome that it contains, this portal is very characteristic of Fischer and was clearly developed from the triumphal arch of the Viennese city council of 1690 [8]; however, in accordance with its special function within the whole façade of the building, its relief is flatter and its proportions more slender. In front of the façade Fischer placed an oval horse-pond, with a statue of a horse-breaker on a high pedestal supported by heavy volutes in the middle of it. This centre group was originally orientated towards the central axis of the portal of the stables. The compact shape of the pedestal and the bizarre outline of the group, together with the richly ornamented railings round the curved basin, form a striking con-trast with the comparatively sober, almost square façade of the stable building. Fischer disguised the face of the cliff with a low façade (which has since been somewhat changed) and the curved shapes of the horse-pond stand out boldly against the blind arches on the ground storey decorated with frescoes of horses. This arcade leads on to the third side of the square, the medieval façade of the Bürgerspital. Fischer's response to the problem of the layout of the square shows great sensitivity to the given conditions: within the rather limited space available, his urbanistic planning achieved a genuine Baroque compromise between the cliff and the town, between the needs of the Archbishop to manifest his rank and status and the social demands of the citizens, and finally, between medieval and Mannerist architecture.

His first church building presented him with a similar problem of town planning. In 1694 the Archbishop decided to build a new 'priests' house' for alumni, old priests as well as students of the two colleges founded by him for noblemen and commoners respectively, together with a church dedicated to the Holy Trinity (Dreifaltigkeitskirche). The sloping site was situated between the first city wall and the palace built by one of his predecessors, Archbishop Paris Lodron, on the right bank of the river Salzach below the hill known as the Kapuzinerberg. Here, too, Fischer was confronted with the problem of achieving a reconciliation between the medieval gateway and the Mannerist palace and of creating a spacious square. This square is dominated by the façade of the church which Fischer erected in the middle of the college buildings

18. Dreifaltigkeitskirche (Holy Trinity Church) and colleges, Salzburg, façade

[18]. It is connected with a Roman example of the High Baroque having a similar function: Borromini's Sant' Agnese in the Piazza Navona, which is also positioned between the fronts of houses and related in its effect to a large square [19]. In both churches, the convex shape of the high cupola is contrasted with the concave façade with its convex terraces of steps between the towers. Fischer, however, articulated the façades of the church and the 'priests' house' by means of a uniform system in the manner of mid-seventeenth-century French architecture – a high ground-storey

19. Borromini, Sant' Agnese, Rome

decorated with grooves, double pilasters on the main storey and windows of very simple shape. In this way, he succeeded in tying the church much closer into the whole complex of buildings. Yet he avoided any effect of monotony by emphasizing the façade in the manner of the French pavilion system. The projecting pavilions at the corners of the college buildings correspond to the projecting towers and the church is made conspicuous by the lower adjoining parts. The low spires, reminiscent of Guarino Guarini (they were rebuilt in 1818 to the detriment of Fischer's original idea), enlivened the otherwise very uniform line of the roof. Fischer used a contemporary French architectural motif – probably taken from Jules-Hardouin Mansart – which was welded into the concave façade of the church as a portal. Above the high doorway with its single framework, he placed an equally high, round-headed window, flanked by double columns standing on a high projecting pedestal. The monumental quality of the portal contrasts strongly with the

concavity of the façade, the convexity of the dome, and the undulating lines of the crowning storey of the towers.

It is clear from the ground-plan of his first church building [20]
that Fischer was trying to achieve a balance between a longitudinal
and a central scheme. To do this he introduced the oval, placing
its long axis at right angles to the façade to form the major axis of

20. Dreifaltigkeitskirche   21. Vignola, Sant' Anna
(Holy Trinity Church), plan   dei Palafrenieri, Rome, plan

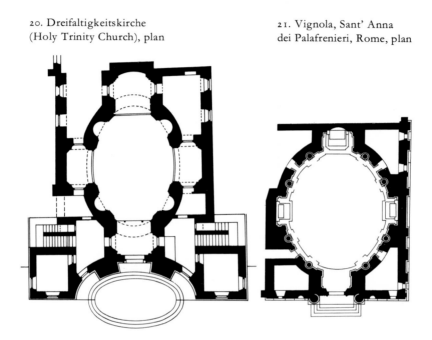

the church. He derived this architectural scheme – the oval with
four annexes attached in the main axes – from Italian Mannerism
(e.g. Sant' Anna dei Palafrenieri in Rome by Vignola, begun 1572
[21]). He developed it, however, by enlarging the four annexes
into the four barrel-vaulted arms of a cross. In this way he brought
out clearly the idea of a longitudinal plan penetrating the oval.
The 'layered' structure of the walls of the church is also in accordance with the principles of Italian Mannerism. An order of giant
Corinthian pilasters seems to overlap an order of smaller Ionic
pilasters behind it [22]. Niches with sculptured decorations, frescoes
(of which only the frames survive), large windows, galleries enclosed by balustrades, altars and the pulpit, designed by Fischer
himself, all serve to break up the flat surface of the walls. Only the
structural parts of the walls, with sharply cut profiles and many
moulded cornices, project. The illusionistic ceiling fresco in the
cupola [23], seeming to open its vault to heaven, depicts the

Virgin's coronation by the Holy Trinity surrounded by choirs of angels and saints, in a composition of a series of concentric circles. What Fischer accomplished here was a striking realization of the idea of the church interior as a total work of art *(Gesamtkunstwerk)*, providing thus an exemplar for the Austrian Baroque of future years. The church was completed in 1702. The architectural elements belong to Italian Mannerism, to the Roman High Baroque, and to the French seventeenth-century style of architecture. In this way Fischer succeeded in establishing a link with contemporary European architecture in Salzburg, where most buildings had hitherto been designed in accordance with north Italian Mannerism.

Shortly after the project for the Holy Trinity Church (Dreifaltigkeitskirche), Fischer designed three other churches for Salzburg. The Archbishop succeeded in doing what his predecessors

22. Dreifaltigkeitskirche (Holy Trinity Church), interior

23. Dreifaltigkeitskirche (Holy Trinity Church), interior of cupola

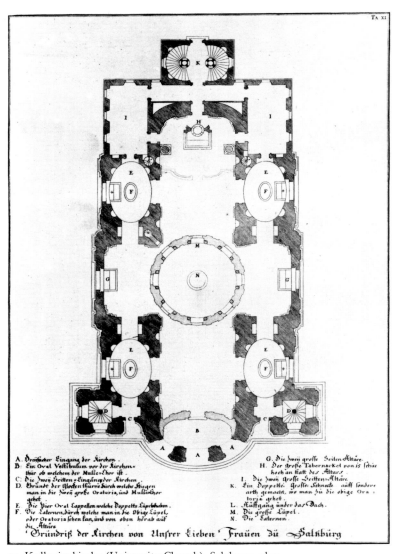

24. Kollegienkirche (University Church), Salzburg, plan

had planned to do but failed to achieve, namely, build a church
for the Benedictine University. The plans for the Kollegienkirche
were ready by 1694 and the foundation stone was laid in 1696. In
building this church Fischer had not only to deal with the problem
of shaping a town square, he had also to add a new accent to the
skyline of the city by confronting the cathedral with another church
of equal importance. To judge from the ground-plan [24], it is
obvious that Fischer was again striving to achieve a synthesis
between the longitudinal and the central scheme, an idea that had
preoccupied the architects of the Counter-Reformation since the

building of Vignola's Jesuit church, Il Gesù, between 1568 and 1584 in Rome. Santino Solari had adopted this idea in his re-building of Salzburg Cathedral between 1614 and 1628 – the first building to be constructed in imitation of Il Gesù beyond the Alps. Further development of this idea resulted in increasing emphasis being placed on the centre of the building, in a ground-plan in the form of a Greek cross with a cupola surmounting the intersection, and in the longitudinal direction being stressed by oval-shaped side chapels in the diagonal axes of the cross. (Artistic theory of the Counter-Reformation rejected the idea of a purely round building for liturgical reasons.) Fischer's Kollegienkirche followed this pattern, which had been first developed by the Early Roman Baroque. It is to some extent reminiscent of Rosato Rosati's

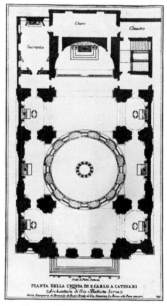

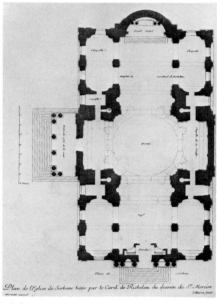

25. Rosato Rosati,
San Carlo ai Catinari, plan

26. Jacques Lemercier,
Sorbonne Church, plan

San Carlo ai Catinari of 1611 in Rome [25], but the proportions of Rosato's church have been changed in favour of those of seven-teenth-century French architecture. It was certainly not by chance that the ground-plan of the University Church of Salzburg was similar to that of Jacques Lemercier's Sorbonne Church in Paris, built after 1635 [26]. The Benedictine University of Salzburg was very proud of its connections with the University of Paris. As an outward sign of this close link, in 1697 the Archbishop solemnly introduced the practice, which had taken place for two centuries at the Sorbonne, whereby every new doctor took an oath on the

27. Kollegienkirche (University Church), façade

Immaculate Conception. The University of Salzburg had distinguished itself both in its reverence and in its theological defence of the doctrine of the Immaculate Conception. The Immaculate Virgin was also the patroness of the new church – she floats over the gable of the façade and in the apse over the high altar. The ground-plan of the church with its four great chapels of equal size was also iconologically motivated – these chapels were dedicated to the patrons of the four faculties. Fischer probably intended the two huge columns in front of the high altar [30] to be a reminder of Solomon's Temple, at the entrance to which stood two pillars, Jachin and Boaz, the symbols of divine omnipotence (1 Kings vii, 15). Their presence stresses the basic idea of this church as a temple of wisdom. Similarly, the towers [29] bear the statues of the four evangelists and the four Church Fathers.

Fischer's original plan for the façade was a flat surface with two towers, in the local tradition of north Italian Mannerism. The most monumental expression of this kind of façade in Salzburg was the west front of the Cathedral, built in the first quarter of the seventeenth century. In his later plans, however, Fischer added an oval porch which was ultimately incorporated into the façade by the pronounced convex curve of the whole central section [27]. In this

28. Kollegienkirche (University Church), Salzburg, view from Mönchsberg

29. Kollegienkirche (University Church), tower

way, he transformed a Mannerist façade into a High Baroque façade. This front now consists of separate, dynamically accentuated masses which are joined together to form a single and picturesque whole. This is achieved by various means: by the counteraction of the giant pilasters and the wall structure which becomes less monumental the higher the eye rises; by the delicate ornamentation reminiscent of Borromini, and by the bizarre shapes of the crowning storey of the towers, derived from Guarini. The back and sides of the church are hardly decorated at all and seem to rise up like crystal blocks to the dome [28]. The peaceful outline of the high dome between the dynamic contours of the towers, crowned with balustrades and statues like diadems [29], is visually related in its effect to the cityscape.

The very lofty interior [30] with its barrel-vaulted nave and transept, above which the light-filled dome appears to float, has an archaic aspect. The structure of the walls, made up of giant

30. Kollegienkirche (University Church), interior

pilasters on high pedestals, is reminiscent of Michelangelo's plans for St Peter's. A wider interval, corresponding with a side chapel, is always flanked by two narrower intervals, in which are set two niches with statues, one above the other. The parapets of the galleries project like balconies above the entrances to the side chapels – this is an architectural feature which can also be observed beneath the dome of St Peter's and which had already been used in Salzburg Cathedral. The oval-shaped side chapels have flat cupolas with round openings in the centre; above them are the galleries, which are also joined together. The high altar is unconventional: it corresponds to the enormous height of the church interior, and it is formed from the whole wall of the apse, framed by huge Palladian columns. Originally a great tabernacle, more than sixteen feet in height and built in the shape of a round temple [31] –

31. Design for tabernacle of Kollegienkirche (University Church)

probably intended to portray the Temple of Solomon – was placed
behind the altar table. (The present high altar dates from 1734.)
In the stucco-work on the wall of the apse the Immaculate Virgin
floats above the globe of the world in triumph over evil and surrounded in luminous glory by angels and clouds. The total impression made by the interior of the church is ultimately determined by
the contrast between the relatively dark nave with its heavy, lofty
barrel-vaulting and the altar space, bathed in light and accentuated
by the silhouettes of the huge framing columns. The elegant stucco
decoration of the interior was also designed by Fischer. He did
not intend the vaulted roof and dome to look as sober as they do
now but the decoration of the vault with frescoes was never
actually carried out. The church was dedicated in 1707, but the
death of the Archbishop delayed the work of decorating and
furnishing the interior. It was not until the present century that
statues were placed in the niches.

Fischer also designed the complex of the hospital of St John
(Johannes-Spital), together with its church, at about the same
time as he was planning the Kollegienkirche. The left wing of this
hospital, the men's ward, was already finished in 1695. The right
wing, the women's ward, was occupied in 1703, but the church
was not dedicated until 1704. The hospital, which is situated
outside the centre of the city beyond the Mönchsberg, is a 'utility'
building. As in the case of the 'priests' house' [18], the church
façade is the central feature of the complex of buildings, which are
a system of pavilions in the classical French manner. The hospital
building is essentially simpler in its structure than the 'priests'
house', but the pavilions gain in emphasis because of their steeply
inclined roofs. The church, which is dedicated to St John the
Baptist, the Archbishop's patron saint, is in many respects a smaller
edition of the University Church (Kollegienkirche). It does, however, contain many new features because of its relationship with
the Roman church of the same name, St John Lateran. The façade
[34] with its open porch and loggia and its receding pediment
recalls Domenico Fontana's transept façade (1586), behind which
two medieval towers rise. The ground-plan [32] reveals that Fischer
even used elements from the early Christian Oratorium Sanctae
Crucis at the Lateran Palace (pulled down in 1586, but known
to us through drawings and engravings [33]) – the corners of the
walls in which the entrance and the altar are situated are based on
the pattern of this chapel. Fischer consciously refrained from
decorating the interior [35] with paintings. The effect is achieved
by the harmonious proportions, the exquisitely shaped Borrominian decoration – a special feature being the motif of the vase
placed in an oval niche – and the pulpit, altars, and other church

32. Hospital church
of St John the Baptist, plan

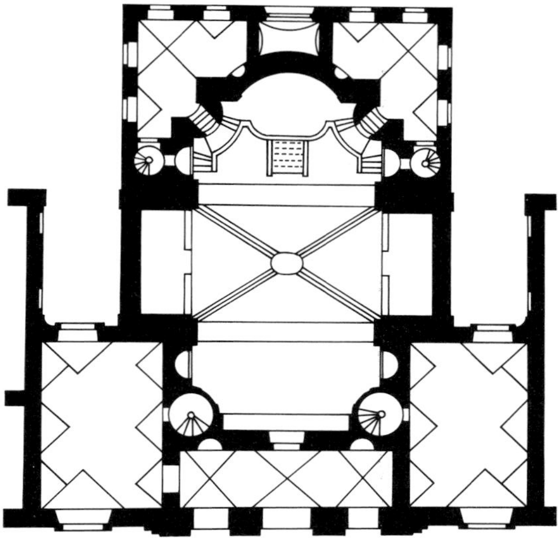

33 (*below left*). Oratorium Sanctae Crucis,
plan and section

34 (*below right*). Hospital church
of St John the Baptist,
design for elevation of façade and interior

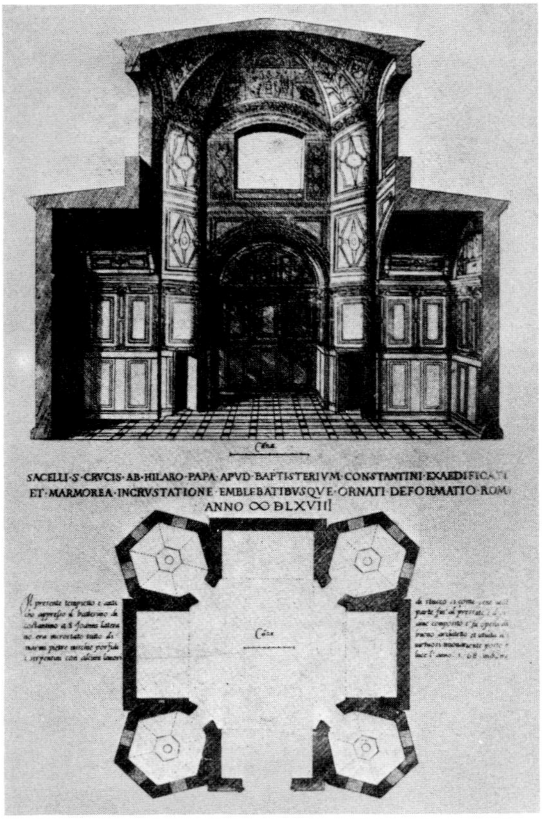
SACELLI·S·CRVCIS·AB·HILARO·PAPA·APVD·BAPTISTERIVM·CONSTANTINI·EXAEDIFICA
ET·MARMOREA·INCRVSTATIONE·EMBLEBATIBVSQVE·ORNATI·DEFORMATIO·ROM
ANNO ∞ DLXVIII

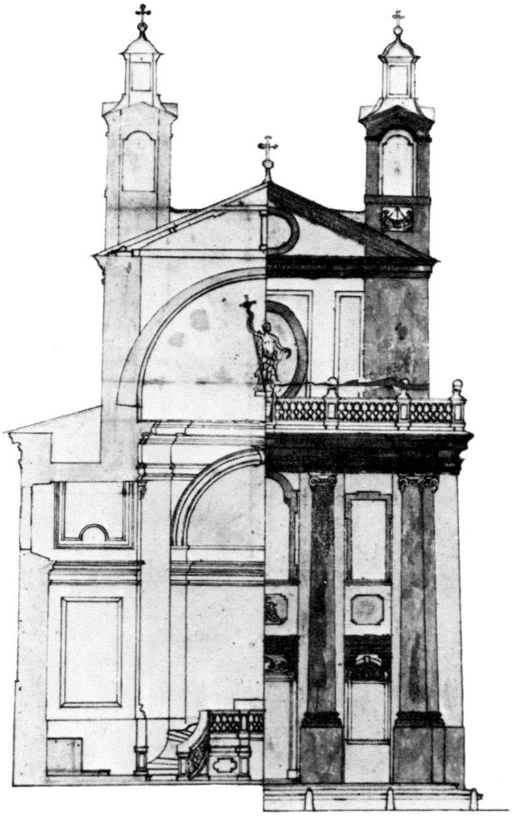

furnishings in red and grey marble, which were designed by Fischer himself and which form part of the structure of the inner walls.

Maria Kirchenthal, the pilgrimage church in the Salzburg mountains near Lofer which was founded by the Archbishop and his family, was built to Fischer's design between 1694 and 1701. The façade with its twin towers follows a north Italian Mannerist scheme which was still customary for Austrian and south German pilgrimage churches at the period (e.g. Maria Plain, near Salzburg). The plan of Fischer's church consists of a square with a smaller

36. Pilgrimage church of Maria Kirchenthal

rectangular annex on each of its four sides – an ancient Roman idea taken up again by Leone Battista Alberti in his design for the church of San Sebastiano at Mantua. Fischer managed to achieve the effect of a monumental central space by using giant pilasters and continuous cornices in all parts alike. The exterior, on the other hand, is almost without decoration and gives the impression of one large block. There can be no doubt that the church was conceived with the surrounding countryside in mind – it was intended to be seen from a long way off in the middle of the mountains, as a testimony to the faith and hope of the pilgrims [36].

The last church Fischer designed for the city of Salzburg was the Ursulinenkirche, built for the sisters of the order of Saint

37. Ursulinenkirche, Salzburg, view from above

Ursula (1699–1705) on the banks of the Salzach. The site available
was in the form of a trapezium, bounded on one side by the river
and on the other by a narrow street running along the foot of the
Mönchsberg. Between this site, the houses at the foot of the cliff,
the city gate and the river wall of the city (which has not been
preserved), there was a triangular space, to which Fischer gave a
pleasant prospect by his church façade [37]. He seems to have
been inspired by the two churches built on narrow, trapezoid
sites at the entrance to the Roman Corso, dominating the Piazza
del Popolo and at the same time providing handsome façades on
the Corso. Fischer used the narrow site in a very similar way, by
allowing the porch of his church with its high pediment to protrude

38. Ursulinenkirche, interior

and the towers to recede behind the flat surface of the front. This
front varies with the central section of the flat façade in the first
plan for the University Church. The towers of the Ursuline Church
have a double function: they form part of the main façade and at
the same time terminate the front, giving onto the river bank
and the street. They are articulated by the oval windows which
were traditionally used in Salzburg at the time and which were, of
course, derived from north Italy. The church also has two clear
functions in the town planning of Salzburg. In the first place, it is
the dominant feature in the triangular space bounded by the city
gate, the cliff and the river bank, and divides the traffic into two
streams. Secondly, if the city is viewed from the opposite bank
of the river, this church forms the corner-stone of a grandiose
panorama. As in the case of the Church of St John the Baptist
Fischer's basic plan was that of a Greek cross with short transepts
and, as in the University Church, with a cupola above the intersection. A system of giant pilasters mounted on high pedestals encircles
the interior [38], as at Maria Kirchenthal. The vaulting is covered
with plant ornamentation, which leaves very little room for decorative painting. Garlands adorn the galleries for the nuns beside
the high altar, the pulpit is supported by *putti*, and angels hold up
the crowned medallion of faith above the sounding-board of the
pulpit. In the richness of its decoration the interior is unique in
Fischer's architecture.

Fischer designed a star-shaped chapel to be built near Salzburg,
but the plan was never carried out. This chapel was to have had
five entrances and five altars [39] and was to be constructed as a
regular pentagon mounted on a circular plinth. The round shape

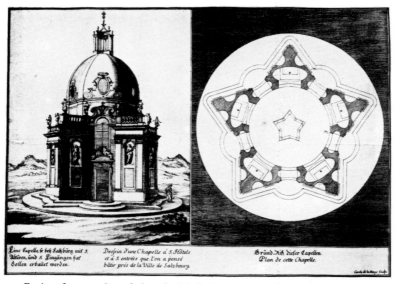

39. Project for star-shaped chapel of St John Nepomuk, view and plan

of the dome was to rise above this pentagon and be crowned with a pentagonal lantern. This very unusual basic plan appears to have been symbolically motivated. The chapel was, it is believed, to have been dedicated to the national saint of Bohemia, John Nepomuk. (The family of Archbishop Thun possessed a great deal of land and property in Bohemia and the saint was venerated everywhere in and around Salzburg.) The story is that after the martyr of the secret of the confessional had been thrown from the bridge in Prague to drown in the waters of the Moldau (Vltava), five stars appeared above the river. The saint is consequently always depicted with a garland of five stars around his head. The apparently iconological basis underlying the shape of the chapel was, however, also very much in accordance with Fischer's architectural ideas at the time. In about 1694 he designed a series of garden pavilions [59, 60], each of which was basically composed, like a regular geometrical figure, of simple geometrical forms, as well as a Landgebäude (country seat) in the shape of a star [58]. The designs of these garden pavilions and the chapel are probably preliminary drawings for the series of engravings of the Archbishop's buildings which was not completed after his death. Like this series, the star-chaped chapel remained an unfulfilled project.

The basic plan of the chapel that he built at Schloss Frain (Vranov) in Moravia between 1698 and 1700 clearly emerged from these and similar ideas [40]. The arrangement of three oval-shaped spaces around a circular central space with a dome in the manner of a triangle circumscribing the circle may also be symbolical, since this chapel is dedicated to the Holy Trinity. Fischer inserted three more oval spaces into the central axes of the sides of the equilateral triangle and these oval spaces are closed off against the central space. He thus achieved a similar wall formation on all sides of the exterior, which is accentuated by the projection of the oval spaces. Three principles that predominate in most of Fischer's work are clearly illustrated in this chapel. First, smaller spaces of a similar kind are arranged around a central space without their outlines being fragmented. Second, the interior of the building is to some extent conceived first and this leads on to the conception of the exterior, so that the arrangement of individual spaces within is visible outside. Thirdly, the whole building is conceived in the context of its natural surroundings, with the intention of giving a higher meaning to this environment [6, behind right].

In Salzburg Fischer had a unique opportunity to practise town planning. He solved four problems connected with squares in the city and by his church buildings gave a new image to the city as a whole. His buildings made High Baroque Roman architecture and classical French architecture familiar to the citizens of Salzburg

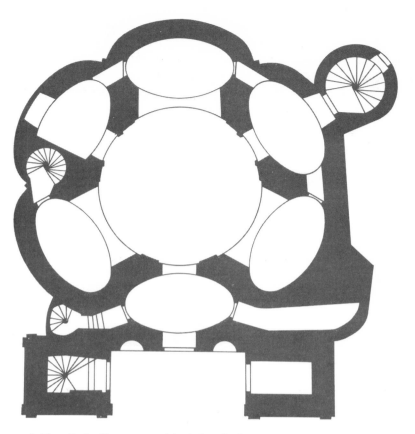

40. Schloss Frain, Vranov, sepulchral chapel, plan

without introducing an alien note into the environment, because they grew organically from the accepted tradition of building there, in other words, the north Italian Mannerist style. Here is the root of Fischer's increasing interest in the Palladian style, which ultimately led to his designing a palace near Salzburg, Schloss Klesheim, as a Palladian villa [66].

The Archbishop's foundations were on such a grand scale that Fischer was able to try out his ideas about church architecture in many different commissions. Each one of his church buildings has its own special quality, which was in turn determined by the demands made by its situation in the city or the surrounding countryside and by its particular function. What is common to all of them, however, is the architect's attempt to achieve a balance between the longitudinal and the central scheme. They also share many other common characteristics. Their ground-plans show that they are all composed of clearly defined forms. The interiors of all these churches are of a monumental character, with giant pilasters on high pedestals and walls split up into several layers articulated by the bold projection of the cornices. Altars and pulpits harmonize with the architecture as well as the decorations of shell and plant motifs. Fischer called the ornamentation which he used in most of his Salzburg churches 'French foliage'. It was a development of Roman High Baroque decoration, especially that of Pietro da Cortona, whose work he had studied in Rome under Johann Paul and Philipp Schor, but mingled with several motifs derived from Borromini. Like the ornamentation employed by the Schors, Fischer's was closely related to that used by Jean Le Pautre, the French architect, and his followers. (The connections between Italian and French ornamentation have not yet been clarified.) This ornamentation enlivens the monumental structure of Fischer's façades and interiors with dynamic, curving lines. Nonetheless, it is true to say that Fischer was in general very sparing in his use of ornament, so as not to detract too much from the great architectonic forms of his churches.

As I have indicated, the differences between these churches are greater than their similarities. The elegant curves of the Drei-faltigkeitskirche (Church of the Holy Trinity), in the midst of the sober and matter-of-fact façade of the 'priests' house' [18], must have had the effect of a small revolution on the people of Salzburg. Those who entered the restrained but monumental portal and saw the clear oval shape of the small though exquisitely pro-portioned and decorated interior, surmounted by its dome which seemed to open the church to the sky – or perhaps, more appro-priately, to heaven – must have been still more powerfully moved. The Dreifaltigkeitskirche was, after all, the first church in Salzburg to be consistently designed by an artist as a total work of art in the Baroque style [22, 23].

How different from this church is the University Church, with its heavy blocks dominating the University and the town! It clearly stands as a rival to Salzburg Cathedral, a rival in Baroque curves [27, 28]. Fischer wanted his version of a harmonious and monu-mental interior [30], a total work of art designed in the modern style, to provide a striking contrast with the multiplicity of forms characterizing the interior of the Mannerist Cathedral. It was ultimately from his ideas for the Church of the Holy Trinity and the University Church in Salzburg that Fischer's most important church building, the Karlskirche in Vienna, developed [91, 96].

It is not surprising that the pilgrimage church in the country, the hospital church, and the Ursuline nuns' church are more closely bound to the architectural tradition of the region. Both the hospital and the Church of St John are more 'spartan' in their structure and decoration. The church does not stand out from the façade of the hospital and its porch doubles as the connecting passage between the parts of the hospital [34]. There is no painting on the interior walls and the ceiling – three colours, white, grey and red, predominate. The interior is small and simple, but it is distinguished by the noble elegance of its lines [35]. The church of the Ursuline nuns, on the other hand, is much more splendid in exterior form and interior ornamentation. Situated at an important point in the plan of Salzburg, it was necessary for the church to have a fine appearance from whichever side it was viewed [37]. Its interior is the most richly adorned of all Fischer's buildings – it is as though he wanted to express in his decoration of the church the sense of purpose, the dedication and the joy with which the sisters set about their task of education [38].

Without any doubt, Fischer's boldest idea was his plan for the star-shaped chapel [39], which was obviously intended to be a monument in the surrounding flat countryside, visible from a long way off and an object of pilgrimages, similar to Maria Kirchenthal with its two towers in the mountains [36]. What Fischer was reviving in his design of the 'star chapel' was the concept of the Italian High Renaissance – based in turn on an antique idea – of a church built on an absolutely regular ground-plan and having exactly the same appearance from whichever point it was viewed. But, like so many Renaissance designs for centrally planned ideal buildings, Fischer's 'star chapel' did not proceed beyond the planning stage. For liturgical reasons, such a building, whether for use as a parish or a monastic church, could not be permitted in that period. It was only possible for Fischer to realize such an ideal plan in a mausoleum [40] – where it was justified in reminiscence of the early Christian *martyria*. Characteristically enough, this sepulchral chapel was built for the Althann family – the members of which had already shown a deep understanding of Fischer's 'neo-Roman' architecture [4, 6].

c. 'Roman' Town Palaces in Vienna

Salzburg was not the only place where Fischer was employed in the last decade of the seventeenth century. While the Archbishop of Salzburg was providing him with opportunities for building churches and for town planning, various Viennese noblemen were giving him commissions to rebuild their town houses and to erect 'pleasure houses' for their recreation outside the city. There was a great shortage of building sites within the city walls and if a nobleman wanted to have a new house built for himself, he usually acquired several smaller properties of common citizens, often dating back to the Middle Ages, and had them reconstructed as a town palace indicative of his status.

The first commission of this kind that Fischer received (in 1692 or 1693) was from the Court Chancellor, Theodor Althet Heinrich Graf Stratmann, who had purchased four houses near the Church of the Minorites (Minoritenkirche). In his first monumental building in Vienna, Fischer was very keen to provide a model of his new architecture and to express his concept of a palatial façade [41].

Prospectus Palatii Comitis Leopoldi de Windischgraz a Palatium Comitissae d. Stratmann.   Prospect des Hoch-Gräffl. Leopold von Windischgrätz Pallasts ut der vordern Sehe. tenstraß a Der Verwittiblen Gräffin von Stratmann Bauß.

41. Palais Stratmann, Vienna, façade

(This palace, which now houses the Hungarian Embassy, was later radically altered by rebuilding and extensions.) Underlying Fischer's concept of the Palais Stratmann were the façades of palaces built by Italian Mannerist architects following Michelangelo, but Fischer added a High Baroque motif – the portal with a central window placed above the door. As in French buildings of the mid-seventeenth century, the ground floor was rusticated, but the rest of the façade was decorated with architectural motifs common in seventeenth-century Austria and, especially in the upper storey, with dramatic sculpture. By this very synthesis, by his independent and individual refashioning of previous examples, Fischer succeeded in overcoming the tendency towards provincialism in Austria, while simultaneously creating a distinctively Austrian Baroque palace façade. The front of the Palais Stratmann in Vienna had many features in common with the façade of the Salzburg 'priests' house' [18], which Fischer was designing more or less at the same time, and the portal of the palace was in many respects closely related to that of the Archbishop's stables at Salzburg [16]. In accordance with its function of manifesting the Court Chancellor's status, however, the Viennese façade was more monumental in structure and much richer in decoration. A motif which Fischer had developed from Borromini's portal of the Collegio di Propaganda Fide in Rome gave emphasis to the central axis. Like Borromini's portal, Fischer's contrasted concave and convex forms, but the arrangement was reversed in Fischer's portal, so that the more monumental motif was used for the door and the lighter one for the window above it. Borromini's door and windows break up the central part of the façade; but Fischer's design is less assertive. The 'diadem arch' over the door he developed from his triumphal arch of the Viennese city council of 1690 [8]. This 'portal and window group' (a door flanked by columns and closely connected with an above window flanked by pilasters, screened by a balustrade and surmounted by a rich pediment), created here, was a feature Fischer was to use again and again, with variations, in his later work. It had a considerable influence on later Austrian and especially on Viennese Baroque architecture. A vestibule with three aisles lay behind the portal of the Palais Stratmann, but nothing is known about the rest of the interior. In its basic design, the vestibule clearly points the way to those of Fischer's later palaces, Batthyány and Trautson [47, 78].

A year or two later, in 1694 and 1695, Prince Eugene of Savoy bought several houses in the Himmelpfortgasse in Vienna and Fischer must have designed the façade of the new Town Palace, which contained seven bays, shortly afterwards. By 1698 the painters were already at work on the ceiling frescoes, but four years later, in 1702, Fischer was no longer in the Prince's service, having been replaced by Johann Lucas von Hildebrandt, who remained Eugene's permanent architect. The Prince's rapid rise in political and military spheres made it necessary for him to enlarge his winter residence. After more houses had been purchased, Hildebrandt added five more bays to the east (1708–9) of Fischer's palace and, many years later (1723–4), another five to the west. In this he copied Fischer's façade – but with fluted pilasters. (This palace is now the seat of the Austrian Ministry of Finance. The features that have been preserved from Fischer's period are the façade, the entrance hall, the staircase, and the ceiling frescoes in two of the rooms.)

Fischer included Prince Eugene's Town Palace – the most important of his town palaces – in his history of architecture [42], in order to prove that he was the author. The palace is reproduced in this book as the scene of an historical event – the solemn audience granted to an envoy of the Grand Vizier of Turkey on 9 April 1711 by Prince Eugene, the President of the Hofkriegsrat (War Council of the Court). In this illustration the palace has twelve bays corresponding to its actual appearance in 1711, including Hildebrandt's first extension. From the description added to it, we may perhaps conclude that Fischer himself had originally designed a palace with twelve bays, although he had to content himself with building only seven because of the original limitation of the site.

42. Town Palace of Prince Eugene of Savoy, Vienna, façade

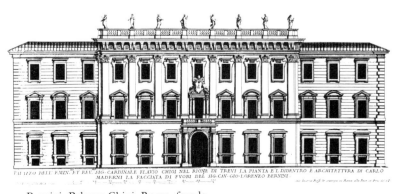

43. Bernini, Palazzo Chigi, Rome, façade

44. Town Palace of Prince Eugene of Savoy, main entrance

The narrowness of the street made it impossible for Fischer to articulate the façade by means of projecting parts [42]. He therefore combined the general scheme of a Roman High Baroque palazzo with elements from seventeenth-century French architecture. By the use of a wealth of architectural motifs the flat surfaces were given a strong rhythm. The wall relief is relatively flat, but is enlivened by the horizontal articulation of the entablature running along the top and by the rich sculptured decoration. Fischer's model was the seven central bays of Bernini's façade of the Palazzo Chigi, facing the church of the SS. Apostoli in Rome [43]. He placed this façade, with its giant pilasters embracing both the main and the upper storeys, on a high rusticated 'pedestal storey' with three rows of little windows, as in French Baroque architecture. He also inserted French rustication between the pilasters. The idea of the trophies above the windows of the main storey and of the frieze below the cornice was derived from seventeenth-century French military architecture. Even the portal, flanked by reliefs and with heavy consoles below the balcony, is basically a French motif, probably known to Fischer through engravings (for example, François Le Vau's portal for the court of honour at the Château de Lignières, 1656). Its proportions are in accordance with those laid down by François Blondel at the Porte Saint-Denis in Paris (1672). This particular solution to the problem of the portal was a complete novelty in Vienna and is unique in Fischer's work. The decision to construct a portal in this way may perhaps have been taken because of a personal wish on the part of Prince Eugene. His mother was a niece of Cardinal Mazarin and he had been badly treated, even ridiculed, in his youth by Louis XIV, which was why he had fled from France and entered the service of the Emperor. It is possible that the victorious general thought that a triumphal gate in the style of classical French architecture and the trophies of victory customary in France would be a timely and suitable sign of his success on the façade of his Viennese town palace.

In contrast to the flat façade, the entrance hall [45] is long and cavernous; it consists of three compartments and has a flattened vault with a central opening, decorated with plant ornamentation and trophies. A rather dark place, it is marked off from the light-filled courtyard by the outlines of double columns. This is a duplication of the architectural motif that was so dear to Palladio and his followers – sometimes called an 'arch-lintel combination of bays'. (This motif also occurs in Carlo Maderna's courtyard of the Palazzo Chigi in Rome, where it has a similar function.) Beside this vestibule Fischer built a monumental staircase, symmetrically arranged and consisting of three flights, in the smallest of spaces. It is only when one ascends this staircase that one can fully grasp its monumental quality. Going up from the obscurity of the vestibule, one passes between massive atlantes and bizarre railings [46] until one comes to the bright, gaily decorated gallery of the main hall. The lofty, flat ceiling of this staircase is very reminiscent of the *Lichthauben* (literally 'light-domes') of the Gothic houses of the Viennese citizens.

Not only the architectonic features of the façade, but also the sculptured and painted decorations of the whole building, were closely related to the life, attitude and achievements of the owner

46. Town Palace of Prince Eugene of Savoy, staircase

of the house. As in the other buildings belonging to Prince Eugene, the decorative themes that were favoured in this town palace were the myths of Hercules and Apollo. These symbolized the Prince's virtue and strength and his advancement of science and the arts respectively. The reliefs on the side of the central gate represent his moral greatness (Hercules and Antaeus) and his patriotic achievements (Aeneas and Anchises). In the staircase, the themes of Hercules and Apollo are combined – there is, for example, a statue of Hercules and there are reliefs above the doors showing the hero's deeds and there is a painting of Apollo in his sun chariot on the ceiling. The labours of Hercules are also shown on the ceilings of the state rooms. At one time, copies of ancient statues of the gods adorned the attic above the façade and consequently the 'Apollo Belvedere' and the 'Hercules Farnese' occupied prominent places among them. In his two extensions of the building, Hildebrandt followed the principle of architectural and iconographical homogeneity.

Bernini's Palazzo Chigi provided the basic idea for the front of another palace built by Fischer [47], this time for the Ban of Croatia, Adam Graf Batthyány. (This palace is situated in the Renngasse near the Schottenkirche in Vienna and is now the property of the Schönborn family.) Here, too, Fischer had to rebuild an earlier complex of buildings. The work was executed between 1699 and 1706. The similarity of its façade structure and iconographic programme with Prince Eugene's palace [42] and its portal and entrance hall with Chancellor Stratmann's [41] reflects the personal lives and the sphere of activity of the owner of the house and his wife. The governor of Croatia had taken an active part in

47. Palais Batthyány, Vienna, façade

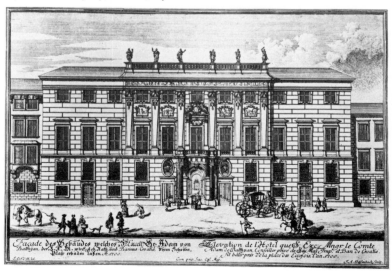

the Prince's campaign against the Turks and his beautiful and gifted wife was the daughter of the Court Chancellor. Prince Eugene had always had very close personal connections with the Stratmann family and later, when they were widows, the Chancellor's daughter and his daughter-in-law became members of his most intimate circle of friends.

The principal effect of the façade of Count Batthyány's palace is made by the contrast between its severe structure and the rich decoration of the central part. Here Fischer took over from Bernini's Palazzo Chigi not only the central section, but also the whole pattern of the façade and, at the same time, he transformed the front according to French principles, decorating it with rustication. He achieved a striking effect of contrast between the rather flat relief of the façade and the convex projection of the portal with its 'diadem arch' and flanking pillars with their concave pedestals and cornices [48] and the central window, a complicated structure of concave and convex forms. A device used on this façade is unique in Fischer's

48. Palais Batthyány, entrance

work – his use of giant pilasters tapering towards the base and embracing two storeys in the central part of the façade. Their capitals are decorated with naturalistic garlands of flowers and *Schabrackenmotive* – motifs reminiscent of saddle-cloths – an ornament derived from textiles but used in a monumental way. The framed reliefs and the frieze (which seems never to have been executed) – in origin Palladian motifs – were derived from French architecture (for example, François Le Vau's façade for the court of the Château de Lignières, 1656). The central doorway, which is a more severe and sober variant of the portal of the Palais Stratmann [41], is basically a motif from Borromini, as are the vases placed in niches above the smaller side-doors (similar to those used at about the same period to decorate the interior of the hospital church of St John the Baptist in Salzburg [35]).

The richly decorated and articulated front is in striking contrast with the monumental simplicity and severity of the vestibule and the completely undecorated courtyard. The vestibule with three aisles on the ground floor of a palace is a theme of the High Baroque and was given perhaps its most monumental form in the Palazzo Barberini in Rome. Fischer used it in the Palais Stratmann and later in the Gartenpalais Trautson [41, 79]. Four pairs of heavy Tuscan columns hold up nine cross-vaults, which are supported at the walls by rusticated pilasters. Above the low, simple, rectangular doors, the motif of the vase set in a high oval-shaped niche is repeated. The symmetrical staircase in three flights, which occupies the whole of the right-hand side of the central area of the house, is, unlike the vestibule, decorated with noble elegance by vases and niches with shell motifs and masks [49]. One is reminded of the sober staircases of seventeenth-century Holland.

Graf Batthyány's virtues and his achievements in war determine the programme of the decoration of the palace – the cavalry battle above the central window, the reliefs planned for the attic frieze, and the reliefs above the windows depicting the labours of Hercules, Aeneas and Mucius Scaevola. It is possible that a deeper meaning was also connected with the *Schabrackenmotive* of the pilaster capitals (perhaps trophies in the war against the Turks?). The house of the governor of Croatia and his wife is, naturally, more modest in its dimensions than the palace of the supreme commander of the imperial forces, Prince Eugene. Nonetheless, in the clarity and elegance of its lines and in the charm of its festive, Borrominian decoration, it is one of the most individual and distinctive of Fischer's palaces.

What the architect was striving to achieve in the fronts of his town palaces built during the last decade of the seventeenth century was a dynamic tension within the façade itself. The narrow streets of the medieval city of Vienna did not allow him to construct strongly projecting central bays, and the flat surface of the walls had therefore to be articulated as far as possible by other means. In the vertical axis Fischer achieved this aim by using a system of giant pilasters and the sculptural 'portal-and-window group' with its complicated curves. Horizontally, the rusticated ground floors had an effect opposite to that of the giant pilasters: they seemed to serve as a high pedestal for the main floor. Their monotonous heaviness is strikingly contrasted with the richly sculptured decoration of the upper storey and the balustrade of the attic with its adornment of statues. The Palais Stratmann [41], with its superimposed double pilasters and the decoration of hollowed-out wall panels on the projecting side wings, is even more closely linked with the type of Viennese architecture common in the seventeenth century. In his design for the façade of Prince Eugene's winter residence [42], Fischer reached a climax in monumentality of form and dynamic tension of decoration. The front of the Palais Batthyány [47], on the other hand, with its emphasis on the central part, points towards the 'Palladian' façades of Fischer's later palaces [76].

d. Garden Palaces, Hunting Lodges, Garden Pavilions, Summer Residences

Fischer was given the greatest possible freedom to exploit his imagination in his garden palaces. During the last decade of the seventeenth century he designed at least eight. They ranged from commissions given to him by the nobility, 'villae suburbanae' at the gates of Vienna, hunting lodges in the Forest of Vienna and in the Marchfeld (the great plain between the Danube and the River March), to the summer residence of Joseph I. He was unable to carry out many of his plans, but later included a number of them in his history of architecture. Several of his designs were used, probably unknown to him, by provincial architects. He also indulged in abstract speculation about ideal ground-plans for small garden pavilions. These ideas have been preserved in a volume of drawings now in the Albertina, Vienna – the Codex Montenuovo. Arranged by Fischer himself, the volume was intended as a pattern book for such 'recreational' architecture. It was in this field that Fischer was at his most original and that his artistic intentions were most vividly expressed.

The Viennese streets were so narrow that the fine façades of the houses could hardly be seen and certainly could not be seen properly. This fact was lamented, for example, by Lady Mary Wortley Montagu, the wife of the English ambassador to the Sublime Porte, in the letters that she wrote when she was passing through Vienna in 1716. However, she praised the suburbs of the city which, she said, consisted entirely of palaces. These suburbs were situated beyond the fortifications, the moat and the 'glacis' – the flat ground, covered with roads and avenues, lying in front of the fortress, on which it was forbidden to build – on the hills round three sides of the city. After the threat of a Turkish conquest had passed, almost every nobleman in Vienna who valued his family's reputation had a garden palace constructed in the suburbs, where he and his family could spend the summer months – this was, of course, in addition to the palace in the city itself. Some noblemen also had hunting lodges built – or restored after the Turks had withdrawn – in the country around Vienna. These hunting lodges were usually splendidly decorated and furnished, not only for the owner's personal pleasure, but also because it was regarded as a special honour if the Emperor accepted an invitation to hunt and his host could give him a worthy reception. It is hardly an exaggeration to say that, after the danger from the Turks had been averted, garden palaces, hunting lodges and country seats sprang up like mushrooms in the suburbs of Vienna and in the surrounding countryside. Fischer, who designed the first of these country houses, set the pattern which prevailed far into the eighteenth century.

In about 1693 he designed one of the earliest of these rather lightly constructed Lustschlösser, which were intended only for short residence, for Ernst Rüdiger Graf Starhemberg, the commander of the defences of the city of Vienna during the Turkish siege. This is the hunting lodge near the village of Engelhartstetten in the Marchfeld. (Taking its name from the estate, it is also known as Schloss Niederweiden. It became the property of Prince Eugene, then passed into the hands of Maria Theresa. It was later radically altered and is now uninhabitable.) Fischer's Lustschlösser were really utopian buildings, idealistic structures from a milder climate than that of Lower Austria. Their flat roofs could not stand up for long against the ice and snow of the harsh Austrian winters. They were the dreams of an architect who wanted to combine the most important achievements in suburban architecture since the Renaissance, the villas of Palladio, and the French garden palaces of the seventeenth century. In his design for Schloss Engelhartstetten [50], Fischer added wings to a pure oval shape in the extension of the shorter axes of this central structure. This basically French type of palace (see, for example, Louis Le Vau's Château Le Raincy [51]), which Fischer also used as a model for the articulation of his façades, was made more dynamic by the Austrian architect's use of Roman High Baroque features. For example, the oval shape projects strongly on both fronts and the dome is concealed by an attic with *œil de bœuf* windows (similar to those in Bernini's design for the Tribuna of Santa Maria Maggiore in Rome [52]) and this is framed

Projpect und Gebäu von Engelhartstetten
Jhro Excell. Herrn Generals Graffen v. Staremberg.

Veue et perspective du Chateau d'Engelhartstetten
de Son Excell: le General Comte de Staremberg.

J. B. Fischer v. E. Rÿm Hoff Ingen. inv.

C. Engelbrecht J. L. Prediet. zu Wien.

50. Schloss Engelhartstetten, front view

51. Louis Le Vau, Château Le Raincy, garden façade

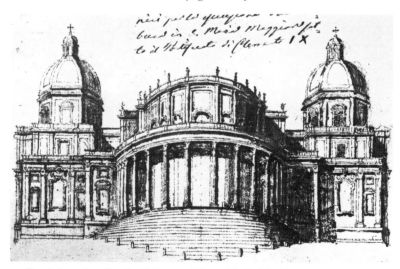

52. Bernini, project for the Tribuna of Santa Maria Maggiore

by concave wings (as in Cortona's façade of the Santa Maria della Pace in Rome). The flat roofs are surrounded by balustrades and were probably intended to be used as terraces from which the hunt could be observed. The palace itself consists of only one storey and was, like a Palladian villa, flanked by detached quadrant wings. (This feature can be compared, for example, with the Villa Badoer at Fratta Polesine and the Villa Trissino at Meledo.) These adjoining buildings, however, were well suited to the French style of the main building. This was in many ways an ideal synthesis and in it Fischer approximated – surely not unintentionally – the Roman and Hellenistic designs for villas that have been handed down to us in Roman murals.

The Lustgebäude or pleasure house – as Fischer himself named this project in his history of architecture – is another variation on the synthesis of a French garden palace with features from the Roman High Baroque (e.g. Bernini's second Louvre project). Here, the oval main hall only projects into the garden, while its dome, towering above the concave middle section of the entrance façade, which embraces a stepped oval platform, provides a striking contrast between concave and convex forms. It is reminiscent of the contemporary façade of the Dreifaltigkeitskirche in Salzburg [18]. Two garden palaces by other architects closely resemble Fischer's project – Schloss Buchlowitz in Moravia (now Buchlovice, Czechoslovakia, built *c.* 1700–1710), and the so-called Meerschein-schloss at Graz in Styria, built before 1708.

Fischer's design for a Lustgartengebäude (pleasure-garden house) intended to stand outside Vienna, but which he did not erect, was much grander both in scale and bearing. It is perhaps the most classical of all his ideas for garden palaces, basically an extension of his Schloss Engelhartstetten design [50], made richer and more monumental by features borrowed from Bernini's first Louvre project [53-5]. The open central pavilion with its giant pilasters and its airy temple-like superstructure has an effect similar to Fischer's reconstructions of Roman and Hellenistic buildings in his history of architecture. Giovanni Battista Alliprandi, employed in Vienna until about 1697, built Schloss Liblitz (now Liblice in Czechoslovakia) for Ernst Joseph Graf Pachta, basing his plans on Fischer's design. Fischer included this project in his history of architecture, calling it a Lust-Garten-Gebäude. It is interesting to note that the original plans of both the merchant Löw's villa in Vienna (now the Palace of the Vienna Boys' Choir in the Augarten) and the Lobkowitz Palace in Prague (built by Alliprandi, 1703-7) were also based on Fischer's design for this garden palace.

In addition to these garden palaces which, despite their utopian features, derived from French *maisons de plaisance* with two main

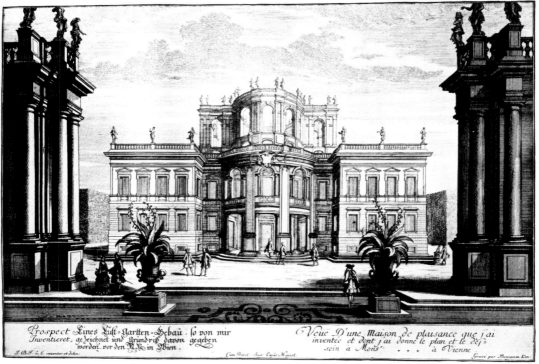

Prospect Eines Lust-Garten-Gebau so von mir
Inventiret, gezeichnet und Grundrisz davon gegeben
worden, vor den N.N. in Wien.

Veue D'une Maison de plaisance que j'ai
inventée et dont j'ai donné le plan et le des=
sein à Mons.... à Vienne.

J.B.F.v.E. inventor et delin.   Cum Privil. Sac. Cæsar. Majest.   Gravé par Benjamin Kea.

53. Project for a Lustgartengebäude (pleasure-garden house)

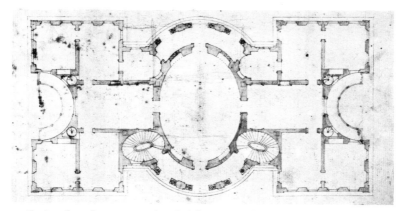

54. Project for a Lustgartengebäude (pleasure-garden house), plan

55. Bernini, first project for the Louvre east façade

façades (facing the garden and the court of honour), Fischer designed a number of other palaces based on unusual and again ideal ground-plans. Only one of them was in fact realized: a palace which, in spite of its very exceptional ground-plan, was provided with two main façades. It was commissioned by the Lord High Steward, Christian Johann Graf Althann, who had it constructed about 1693 in the Roßau, on the banks of one of the arms of the Danube in Vienna. (It was pulled down in 1869 to make way for the Franz-Josephs-Bahnhof.) Fischer took the X-shaped plan [64] from a villa by Serlio, but adapted it to the French conception of the garden palace by arranging the four arms of the St Andrew's cross like the vanes of a windmill around an oval central space. Thereby he provided the two (entrance and garden) façades traditionally found in a garden palace. In the acute angles of the X Fischer placed two octagonal rooms, thus creating two side façades each consisting of a projecting central section flanked by wings – in other words, a design similar to that of the main façades. A symmetrical staircase was placed in front of the entrance façade. On the *piano nobile* there was an oval main hall with its longitudinal axis set at right angles to the oval room on the ground floor. This architectural play with the oval as the central part of a building reminds one of the close affinity between this Viennese garden palace and the small garden pavilions which Fischer was designing for Salzburg at the same time [59, 60]. In the Gartenpalais Althann the deliberately simple, almost monotonous, treatment of the wall surface, which was uniform for the whole exterior, and the clean curve of the high cylindrical attic which concealed the dome made a striking contrast with the complicated ground-plan. It was, indeed, this contrast which gave the building its special charm.

Graf Althann's palace attracted the attention of contemporary architects. Domenico Egidio Rossi somehow obtained the ground-plans and an elevation, which were found among his own designs. Germain Boffrand may well have been indebted to it for his design of the Château La Malgrange, near Nancy (*c.* 1712), built for Leopold Joseph Karl, appointed Duke of Lorraine by the Emperor Leopold I after the Peace of Rijswijck in 1697. It is not certain whether Filippo Juvarra, who began to build the Palazzo Stupinigi near Turin in 1729 on a very similar ground-plan, was acquainted with Fischer's building or whether he based his palace on his own variation of Serlio's plan. The Veltrusy Palace near Prague, which dates from the first half of the eighteenth century, also has a similar ground-plan.

This play with simple geometrical forms on the ground-plan inspired Fischer to design not only garden pavilions and chapels [59, 60, 39, 40], but fortified country seats as well. For a fortress, a regular geometrical figure as ground-plan was traditional. It would appear that the use of fortification in these houses was mere play – yet only a little earlier the owners of such fortified country seats or castles had been obliged to defend themselves inside them. Fischer's most ambitious project of this type was his ideal design for a Grosses Landgebäude (large country house) based on a circular ground-plan and situated on a mountain. (In later literature it is often called the Bergschloss [mountain castle] to avoid confusion with the star-shaped Landgebäude [58].) This grandiose concept was half fortress and half pleasure palace [56]. Several drawings of it have been preserved and Fischer finally used the project as a background to an engraving of two vases in the last book of his

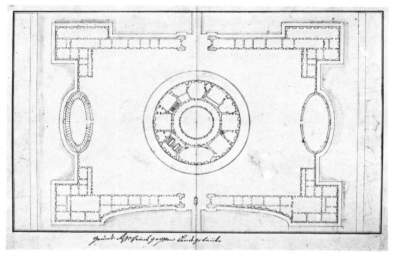

56. Project for a Grosses Landgebäude (large country house), plan

57. Project for a Grosses Landgebäude (large country house), view

history of architecture [57]. The underlying principle was his idea of the Roman 'mole' or mausoleum, which had been in his mind when he was planning – more or less at the same time – the ancestral hall of the mountain castle, Schloss Frain [4, 6], and which he later included in his history of architecture in connection with his reconstruction of the Emperor Hadrian's mausoleum in Rome. The most grandiose example of a castle combining both the qualities of a fort and those of a Lustschloss – Vignola's Palazzo Caprarola near Viterbo – inspired him to make use of a round courtyard surrounded by an arcade. His circular arrangement of spaces with different geometrical forms – squares, ovals and trefoils – was similar to his designs for garden pavilions in Salzburg [59, 60]. The cylindrical palace on a high and entirely unarticulated base had only one entrance, but it was, like a Palladian villa, provided with single-storey wings. Their gateways were developed from Fischer's designs for park gates [2, 3]; their oval pavilions with high attics were intended to be stables. This was altogether an audacious plan, but the palace itself was unfortunately never built. It is, however, worth mentioning that one of the two vases in the style of Jean Le Pautre which form the framework for this palace in Fischer's history of architecture [57, left] was imitated in the park of the Schwarzenberg Palace in Vienna (after 1720) and in the collegiate church at Dürnstein on the Danube (1723).

There can be no doubt that Fischer saw the Mannerist Schloss Stern on the 'White Mountain' near Prague (Letohrádek Hvězda; built in 1555) when he was in Bohemia in 1691. His plan for a star-shaped, fortified Landgebäude [58] follows this pattern. Here, six rhomboids are arranged around a hexagonal central room and separated from one another by rectangular rooms. The two-storeyed building is surmounted by a dome above the central space and a little tower on each point of the basic star shape. The use of a moat and star-shaped bastions follows the Dutch system of fortification that was widespread before Vauban. The only access to the building is over a drawbridge. Fischer included this plan, which again was never carried out, in his history of architecture together with his projects for churches and palaces mainly to show his skill as a military architect. In the formal sense, of course, it is a counterpart to the 'star chapel' of St John Nepomuk [39] but, in the latter case, Fischer transformed the ponderous mass of the Landgebäude into a tall monument which could be seen over a wide area, in accordance with the needs of a pilgrimage chapel.

Among the most interesting of Fischer's plans are those for eight little garden pavilions (one of them dating from 1694) which were probably designed for a pheasantry laid out by the Archbishop of Salzburg in the park of Klesheim. It seems likely that he intended to

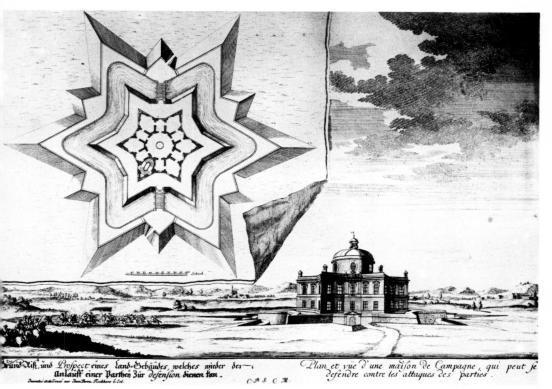

Grund-Riß, und Prospect eines Land-Gebäudes, welches wieder der — Anlauff einer Parthen zur defension dienen kan. C. B. S. C. M.

Plan et vüe d'une maison de Campagne, qui peut je défendre contre les attaques des parties.

58. Project for a star-shaped fortified Landgebäude
(country house), plan and view

publish them in his projected set of engravings of the Archbishop's
buildings. Only one of these garden pavilions was realized, however
– the so-called Hoyoshaus [59] which is still standing in the park of
Schloss Klesheim. The architect's play with simple geometrical
forms in the plan is common to all these designs. He grouped

59. Design for garden pavilion

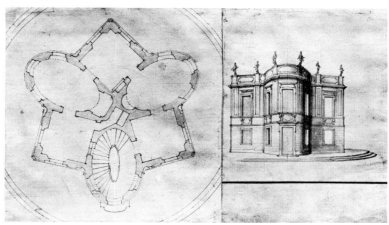

spatial elements of geometrically equal shapes – ellipses, squares, rectangles, hexagons, octagons – in different ways around a central space in such a way that the combination would produce a regular geometrical figure. In the elevations he sometimes emphasized the central hall by crowning it with a 'belvedere'.

Similar types of ground-plan are to be found in late Gothic architecture, and have a religious significance (e.g. the triangle for the Trinity). They had also appeared in late antiquity and thus preoccupied such High Renaissance architects as Leonardo, Bramante and Peruzzi [61] as well as such Mannerists as Serlio [62] and Montano [63]. Sixteenth-century French architects – Du Cerceau, for example, in his designs for palaces – tried their hands at similar solutions. Even as late as the seventeenth century architects continued to show interest in these problems, especially in France – François Mansart's design for the Bourbon chapel at St Denis is a

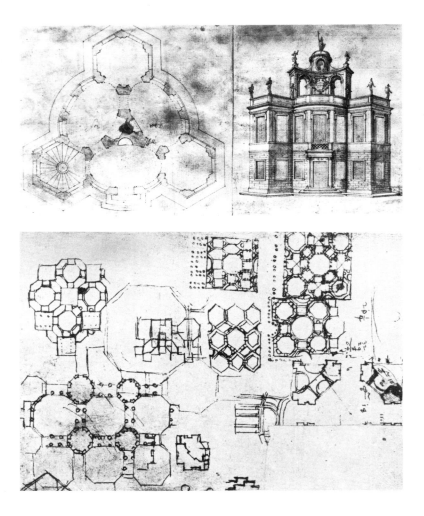

case in point. In Germany, too, there were symbolic ground-plans for chapels dedicated to the Holy Trinity which may perhaps derive from the medieval tradition. Fischer's designs differed from those of Renaissance and Mannerist architects in that he did not make the ideal form of the building's exterior the basis of his consideration. His method was, rather, to conceive his buildings from within, starting from the ideal form of each spatial element, giving preference to the oval. Unlike Borromini and Guarini, in whose work similar tendencies may be seen, Fischer made it a principle to prevent the individual spatial elements from penetrating or fragmenting each other. He wanted to preserve intact the ideal form of each one. In this respect his architectural ideas were close to those of the Italian High Renaissance. Partly because he conceived them from within – but partly also because of their subordinate function – these garden pavilions have few decorations on the exterior. In

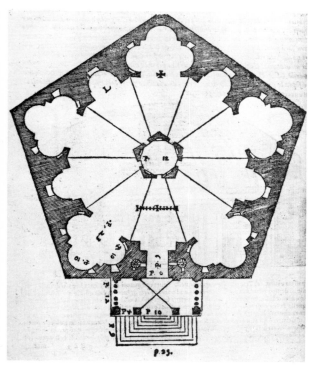

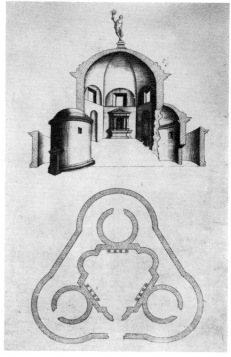

60 (*opposite above*). Design for garden pavilion

61 (*opposite below*). Peruzzi, designs for centrally planned buildings

62 (*above left*). Serlio, pentagonal temple, plan

63 (*above right*). Montano, hexagonal temple with three circular chapels

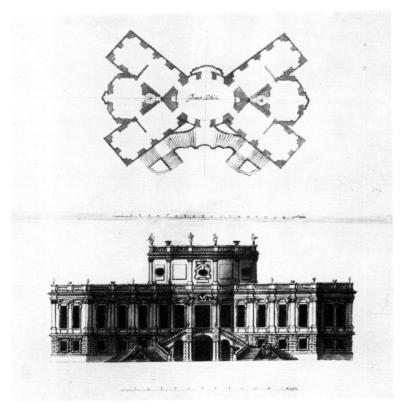

64. Gartenpalais Althann, plan and elevation

style they resemble French façades of the late seventeenth century –
though one of the pavilions has a superstructure in the manner of
Borromini [60].

In these works of minor importance Fischer was able to give
clear expression to his fundamental idea of combining independent
and unfragmented spatial elements. It is apparent in all his free-
standing buildings which present different aspects from different
points of view – his triumphal arches, his garden palaces, the
University Church in Salzburg and the Karlskirche in Vienna. In
this principle he concurred with the theories of French classical
architecture as formulated by François Blondel. It is probably no
coincidence that he chose garden pavilions for this play with
geometrical forms; clipped trees in clear geometrical patterns were
a feature of French parks.

Fischer's idea of combining independent spatial elements without letting them penetrate or merge into each other had a considerable influence on architects in Bohemia (Santin Aichel and
Kilian Ignaz Dientzenhofer) as well as on south German architectural theorists. The ground-plan of Thomas Archer's garden

pavilion for the Duke of Kent (illustrated in *Vitruvius Britannicus*, vol. 1, 1717) provides an interesting parallel with Fischer's designs and should also be mentioned in this context.

Fischer's designs for *fürstliche* summer residences – that is to say summer palaces for sovereigns, whether emperor, king or prince bishop – form an independent group apart from his projects for garden palaces, fortified country seats and smaller garden pavilions. Schloss Schönbrunn [65], built outside Vienna on the banks of the river Wien, retains little of the grandeur of Fischer's first utopian project [9], though it too claims to be a second Versailles. (It was begun in 1696 when Joseph I was King of Rome and not yet completed when he died in 1711 after six years' reign as Emperor.) In the French manner, it consists of a series of pavilions with a simple ground-plan and restrained decoration of the exterior walls. Basically, it derives from Louis Le Vau's project for the garden front at Versailles. In the central section there are six columns, as in Jules-Hardouin Mansart's garden front at Versailles, but the main door is approached by way of a ramp embracing a round basin – a concession to the Roman High Baroque. This central section was crowned by a kind of triumphal gate – a motif recalling Borromini's design for the Palazzo Pamphilj – intended to shelter an equestrian statue of Joseph I which was never put up. The vast court of honour with its two fountains, which was conceived as a setting for the procession of carriages on grand occasions, is flanked by long

65. Schloss Schönbrunn, general view

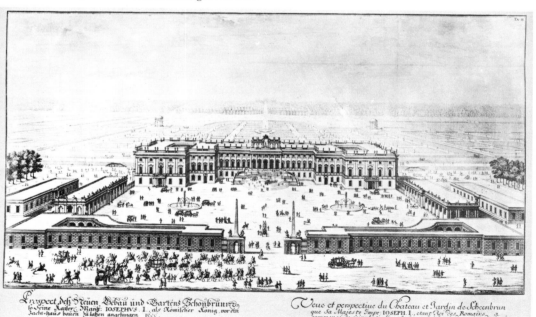

stable-buildings, similar in function to the side wings connecting Bernini's colonnades with the portico of St Peter's. The out-buildings on the river bank (coach-houses and accommodation for the palace staff) had a fortress-like severity. Two obelisks guard the entrance into the court, a motif which may perhaps derive from Strabo's description of the Serapeum in Alexandria. From the relatively narrow terrace in the middle section of the other side of the palace a symmetrical staircase led into the garden, which was laid out in the French style and consisted of a formal parterre bordered by canals and flanked by a pair of small round temples. The park was to have been closed off by colonnades at the foot of the hill known as the Schönbrunner Berg and by a belvedere on its summit (similar to one of the park gates of 1687 [3]), which would have provided a fine view from the palace, but they were never built. There can be no doubt that the palace was not designed simply as a hunting lodge – though Fischer described it as such in his history of architecture [65] – but rather as a summer residence for the young King, who was later to become Emperor. This is indi-cated by the large number of state apartments it contains. In accordance with the court ceremonial, the left wing was dedicated to the King and the right to his consort. The two royal apartments were linked only by the main hall in the centre of the palace, which contained a ceiling painting by Johann Michael Rottmayr glori-fying the house of Austria. A huge symmetrical staircase with three flights of stairs and occupying the whole front of the right-hand pavilion led to the Queen's rooms. The interior of the palace was, however, radically altered by the court architect, Nikolaus Pacassi, during the reign of the Empress Maria Theresa. All that is preserved is Sebastiano Ricci's ceiling fresco for the dining room – an allegorical illustration of the education of a young prince in virtue and continence, leading to his assumption into heaven and his eternal glory. The ceiling on which this fresco is painted is now that of a staircase.

Schloss Schönbrunn is the building in which Fischer came closest to French classical architecture, which was clearly demanded by his patron. The residence of Joseph I, in which Fischer had to observe the ceremonial requirements of the court, is separated by an enormous distance from the architectonic ideas for 'pleasure houses' which were then preoccupying Fischer. Although it was certainly not his most original work, it was, from the sociological point of view, his most important commission up to that time. This is probably why he had engravings made of the design in 1701 and sent these to various influential patrons in Europe. Nowadays, of course, the palace presents rather a different appearance. In 1737 the loggia was removed from the roof and pitched roofs were erected. Pacassi altered the original outside stairs and had a mezzanine floor inserted between the main and the upper storeys. The park was also extended at about this time and the menagerie was laid out. In 1775 Ferdinand Hetzendorf von Hohenberg built on top of the hill the 'Gloriette' in which Fischer's idea of a belvedere lives on.

At Schloss Klesheim, the summer residence that he designed for the Archbishop of Salzburg (begun in 1700), Fischer used architectural ideas derived from the two building stages of Versailles, as he did at Schönbrunn. In Salzburg, however, where the tradition of north Italian Mannerism was so firmly rooted, he was able to attempt a closer connection with Venetian architecture, both in his ground-plan [67], which is very similar to Palladio's Palazzo Chiericati in Vicenza [68], and in the central section of the façade with its superimposed open arcades [66]. The practice of opening the central section of a house completely by means of arcades was occasionally adopted by French classical architects, though only for smaller buildings (e.g. the house of the court painter Charles Lebrun, at Montmorency). Fischer does not seem to have found his immediate model in architecture so much as in north Italian *Cinquecento* painting though, and especially in the airy buildings depicted by Paolo Veronese (e.g. the 'Palladian' villa in the Stanza

66. First project for Schloss Klesheim, front view

Prospect des Neüen Lust-Gebaüdes Sei.
ner Hoch Fürstl. Gnaden zu Salzburg, Clesheimb, oder
die neue Favorite genandt.

Cum Privil. Sacr Cæsar Maj.

Vüe D'une Maison de plaisance de Son
Altesse Mgr. l'Archevéque de Salzbourg, nommée Clesheimb
ou la nouuelle Favorite.

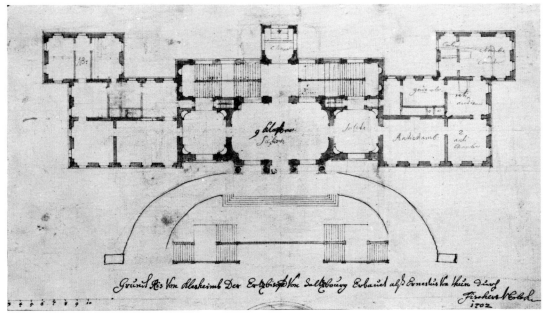

67. Schloss Klesheim, plan

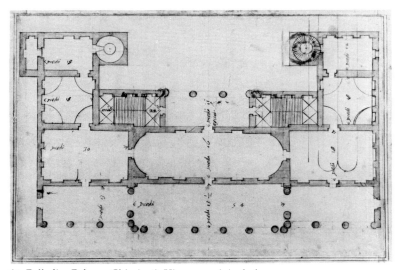

68. Palladio, Palazzo Chiericati, Vicenza, original plan

di Bacco of Palladio's Villa Barbaro, Maser). But Fischer changed these models by allowing the flanks of the central section to project in gentle curves, in the Roman High Baroque manner. Unlike the French garden palace, Schloss Klesheim does not have two main façades onto the court and garden. The visitor approached it, through the garden, on the central axis of the building to the main front, where a ramp gave access to the entrance. The rear façade is not very distinguished architecturally and originally had no access to the garden. This arrangement may have been determined by the site, for the main front of the building was to be seen from both the Hohensalzburg and the Mönchsberg. Inside, a monumental staircase with symmetrically arranged flights filled the whole central projection at the back of the palace. The heavy vaulting of the main hall, with its small, oblong, central opening through which the clearly lighted lantern could be seen, is reminiscent of a Palladian villa. The interior decoration, for which Fischer provided detailed designs, was to have included a great deal of ceiling painting.

This design was ideal and utopian and could not be carried out in an Alpine climate, but Fischer included it in his history of architecture [66]. The palace actually built was a toned-down version of the one originally planned, with smaller windows instead of the open arcade. It makes much more of a French impression than the first design and, because of the different proportions of the windows, the building does not seem to be light and soaring, but very firmly based on the ground. The ramp was later changed.

69. Project for a Gartengebäude (garden house)

Fischer made use of the idea of an open loggia for the central section of a palace in another design for a small Gartengebäude (garden house) [69]. This project, which again was not executed, was to some extent based on the idea of the *Raumtor mit Flügeln*, which was first realized in the Liechtenstein belvedere [1], but is interpreted here as a Palladian villa on a pedestal formed of arcades.

The plan consists of an oblong central hall to which four oval rooms of equal size are joined at the corners. In this, the Gartengebäude is clearly in accordance with Fischer's other designs for small garden pavilions [59, 60]. The oval-shaped spaces however penetrate into the oblong central space, fragmenting it slightly, which is very unusual in Fischer's work. This plan reminds one of the hospital church of St John in Salzburg [32], in which the motif of the arcade with an oval window above is also to be found. Low outbuildings were to have flanked the central structure. The architect also intended it to be surrounded, not by a French park with clipped hedges, but by trees allowed to grow naturally. The fountain in front of the Gartengebäude completed the composition. It consisted of two statues of athletic fishermen standing, without pedestals, on the ground and pulling out of the water a net made of copper wire in which they had caught a dolphin – an unusual Berninesque idea.

Fischer's designs for a Lustschloss (garden palace) for Frederick I of Prussia [70] were to some extent a combination of the palace on the hill, from the first project for Schönbrunn, and a Palladian villa. On arriving at the Berlin court in 1704 Fischer probably presented them as his 'credentials'. He had taken Bernini's second project for the Louvre as his point of departure. As in his first plan for Schönbrunn [9] he combined the huge semicircle of the façade, which enclosed a great basin, with an arrangement of terraces.

70. Design for a Lustschloss (garden palace) for Frederick I of Prussia

The centre of the building includes a Palladian villa which possibly follows the curve of the whole front and has a central section with five bays and tower-like side sections. These sections are connected by low wings to the central part of the building, rather like Palladio's Villa Pisani in Montagnana. The ground floor of the villa consists of open arcades. The wings are articulated like those in the first project for Schönbrunn, but their double columns standing on low pedestals make them resemble late seventeenth-century French architecture more closely. In comparison with Klesheim, the Palladian characteristics are even more pronounced. This is especially noticeable in the final design for the King of Prussia's palace [70]. In the synthesis that he achieved here between Palladianism and the classical French style, Fischer arrived at a solution which has clear analogies with English architecture of the same period.

Fischer had always been interested in architecture in the Palladian tradition. This interest, underlying all his work, can be observed especially in the churches that he built in Salzburg. From about 1700 onwards, however, it became even more prominent in his work – particularly in his designs for garden palaces. Here, the important change in his style, which was to take place after his journey to Berlin, Holland and England, is already anticipated.

e. Altars and Monuments

The little garden pavilions and hunting lodges reveal Fischer's intentions very clearly. The same may be said of his altars and *Scheinarchitektur* for solemn entries and obsequies, which may be grouped under the general heading of monuments. Here, he could give freer scope to his imagination than in his church buildings and palace façades; he could express his favourite ideas without restraint and could give far greater attention to sculpture and ornament.

In 1692 he designed a new high altar for the pilgrimage church of Mariazell in Styria [71], where the miraculous image of the Virgin and Child drew thousands and thousands of pilgrims every year, including even the Emperor's family. Although Fischer directed the work himself, the altar, which cost vast sums of money because so many of its parts were made of precious metals, lost much of the fine harmony that Fischer had given it in his original drawing when it had been completed by all the stonemasons, sculptors, goldsmiths and painters who shared in its construction between 1695 and 1704. Further, the four silver statues beside the tabernacle were melted down during the Napoleonic Wars and replaced by wooden figures.

71. Design for high altar of Mariazell pilgrimage church (detail)

The altar, which is dedicated to the Trinity, represents the
Redemption. The architectonic idea goes back to Bernini's *Cathedra Petri* in St Peter's, and the ornaments recall Johann Paul Schor's decoration of the throne itself. The group of God the Father with the crucifix – a Baroque version of the medieval *Gnadenstuhl* (throne of mercy) – was inspired by Bernini's mystical drawing, diffused in an engraving by Franciscus Spiere under the title 'Sanguis Christi'. Fischer transformed these stimuli in accordance with his original idea of the Liechtenstein belvedere motif [1]. A portion of a centrally planned building is placed in front of a triumphal gate crowned by a 'diadem arch'. This centralized building consists of two rows of columns, producing a complicated arrangement of pedestals and cornices which frame the high arch like a proscenium. In Fischer's drawing, the figures seem to grow out of the dynamism of the semicircular shape, from the vibrant movement of the plant ornament on the pedestals. The mystery of the Redemption is symbolized in dramatic action. Above the altar-table, hewn from a single block of stone, the globe (a silver tabernacle mounted on rocks) seems to hover, encircled by the crown of thorns and dominated by the serpent, the symbol of evil. But salvation comes from heaven above. In a glory of light and worshipping angels the dove of the Holy Ghost appears: God the Father has sent his Son for the redemption of mankind. Like a vision, Christ suffering on the cross floats within the triumphal arch, a mediator between the sinful world and heaven. Directing their thoughts to him, men shall be filled with true compassion, like the Virgin and St John, and determine to imitate him.

Nine years after building his remarkable triumphal arches to celebrate the coronation of Joseph I [7, 8], Fischer erected in the same places in the centre of Vienna and for the same patrons two arches to mark the solemn entry of the King and his bride after their wedding in 1699. His architectural sources were similar – a round temple incorporated in a triumphal arch with three gateways – but his style had in the meantime changed radically. In a word, it had become more classical. The two architectural elements were merged and synthesized to produce the most characteristic motif of Fischer's architecture, the Liechtenstein belvedere motif, governing both storeys. The effect of the arch of the foreign merchants [72] derives from the contrast between the heavy lower storey with its 'diadem arch', carried by atlantes on high pedestals, and the light cloud-borne superstructure which is reminiscent of Hellenistic architecture. This superimposition of a light structure on a heavy base also has an iconographical significance. It would appear as though the King, when passing under the arch, rose upwards through its open roof and was glorified in the image of

the grace-dispensing sun god within a canopy-like temple, surrounded by allegorical representations of his virtues. This apotheosis was not shown as a static picture, but as a process that was
taking place (just as a mystery of faith was transformed into action

Triumphs-Pforte, welche zu Wien von denen Herr: Niederlegern daselbst zum Einzüge und zum Beylager Seiner Weiland Kaiserl: Maij: Josephi I. Ao 1699. erbauet worden.

Arc triomphal, que Mrs: les negotiants étrangers de Vienne y dressérent pour l'entrée et pour les nopces de feu Sa Maj: Imp: Joseph I. l'an 1699.

72 (*opposite*). Triumphal arch of the foreign merchants, 1699

73. Josephssäule (St Joseph's Column)

in the high altar at Mariazell [71]). Fischer deemed this transient structure, designed for a special festive occasion, important enough to form a kind of frontispiece to the fourth book of his history of architecture (the section devoted to his own works). The second of the triumphal arches of 1699, that of the Vienna city council, was based on the same architectural principle but differed from the first in detail as it was dedicated to Joseph's bride. She was represented as rising towards her husband and imperial parents, surrounded by gods and riding in Juno's peacock chariot, which was drawn by allegories of her virtues.

Fischer's project for the Dreifaltigkeitssäule – a column dedicated to the Holy Trinity – on the Graben in Vienna was carried out only in part. But another votive column was built in a different Viennese square in accordance with a design of Fischer's [73]. The Emperor Leopold I had solemnly promised in 1702 to have a column erected on the Hoher Markt in Vienna to his son's patron, St Joseph, on his son's safe return from the War of the Spanish Succession and, even when he was on his deathbed, he made arrangements for his vow to be carried out as quickly as possible. The Josephssäule, a wooden column with a group show-ing the marriage of the Virgin and St Joseph, who were also the patron saints of all Austria, was erected in 1706 in accordance with Fischer's plans. (The present stone column, it should be noted, was built later by Fischer's son, who modified his father's project.) The basis for the original design was the *baldacchino* in the Val-de-Grâce in Paris, which Fischer transformed into a monument by the insertion of a high pedestal for the group of statues and the addition of lateral supports. The different arrangement of the columns and the roof in the shape of a cupola fragment made the *baldacchino* look like the inside of a round temple opening in front of the spectator. The old idea of a votive column was combined with that of a group of figures placed on a high pedestal and sheltered by a *baldacchino*, in such a way that the structure provided different aspects when viewed from different sides. Its effect was enhanced by the architect's conceiving it in close relation to the surrounding square.

Fischer's most ingenious solution to this kind of architectural problem was his high altar erected in 1709 in the Franciscan Church, the parish church of the city of Salzburg [74]. Michael Pacher's shrine-altar was dismantled at this time, but its most important element, the statue of the Virgin and Child which had been venerated as a miraculous image since the Counter-Reforma-tion, was to remain in its place. Fischer showed that he had more respect for Gothic art than the clerical authorities of his time. His altar not only includes Pacher's Madonna but, in its great height,

74. Franciscan Church, Salzburg, high altar

is fully in accordance with the concept underlying the medieval altar and is therefore harmoniously integrated into Hans von Burghausen's Gothic chancel. Fischer also incorporated a number of features reminiscent of Gothic altars, notably the lofty superstructure and the flanking statues – paralleling the *Gesprenge* and the *Schreinwächter* (carved guardians) of the Gothic shrine-altars. Essentially, however, the altar is composed of Fischer's favourite ideas for portals, altars and monuments, which are here perfected. The Liechtenstein belvedere motif is combined with the idea of a monument presenting several different aspects, the whole functioning as an altar which enshrines as well as crowns the miraculous image. The shape of the altar seems to change as it is viewed from different points. Seen from a short distance, the 'diadem arch' seems to be a 'crown' above the statue of the Virgin and the wall behind a back-cloth closing it off; seen from a distance, the illusionistic effect of the wall behind appears to transform the arch into a round temple, the shrine of the image with the dove of the Holy Spirit floating down into it. The original appearance of the altar was dominated above all by the gilt columns and draperies of the statues, which were boldly set off by the grey piers and walls of the chancel. Seen from far down the dark Romanesque nave of the church, the illusionistic effect of the altar in the bright light of the Gothic chancel is perfect. This is one of the few churches in which three architectural styles are happily blended, forming an interior of exquisite harmony. Shortly afterwards, Fischer used the design for the 'diadem arch' of this altar in a slightly altered form for the portal of the Dietrichstein Palace in Vienna (now the Institut Français).

The catafalques which Fischer designed in these years form a group of their own. After the death of Emperor Joseph I in 1711, *castra doloris* were set up according to Fischer's designs in the Augustinian Church and St Stephen's Cathedral in Vienna. Such ephemeral constructions would be erected simultaneously in all the churches, at home and abroad, where solemn obsequies were read after the death of a person of distinction (there was no need for the corpse to be present in them). The practice seems to have originated in the liturgy of the requiem, to which had been added, since the Renaissance, the idea of a Roman imperial triumph as well as elements from Roman funeral rites. There is evidence that large architectural structures began to be built for these ceremonies in the sixteenth century. The practice of erecting huge and very expensive catafalques of wood decorated with painted cloth, statues, draperies and all kinds of ornaments reached its climax in the seventeenth and the early eighteenth centuries, when it spread throughout Europe, even to Protestant countries like England.

78.

75. *Castrum doloris* for Joseph I in St Stephen's Cathedral, Vienna

Fischer's *castrum doloris* (or *Trauergerüst*) in the Gothic Augustinian Church near the Hofburg (the court church where the imperial family worshipped) followed the traditional concept of a canopy above the coffin, apparently influenced by a work of the Berlin court architect Johann Friedrich Eosander, whom Fischer seems to have met on his journey through Prussia. But Fischer's invention surpassed Eosander's in grandeur and was far better incorporated into the church interior. Four pillars of the nave were decorated like Roman triumphal columns – with spiral reliefs representing the Emperor's deeds – and guarded the coffin beneath the canopy like giant sentinels. Behind them the imperial mausoleum seemed to rise, and above it the apotheosis of the Emperor was shown: in a Roman chariot borne by eagles Joseph I seemed to ride to heaven and eternal glory. Needless to say, every part of this construction was rich in iconographical meaning.

The *castrum doloris* in St Stephen's [75], commissioned by Vienna University, was less sumptuous but more 'modern' in invention and style. Fischer took his basic idea from Raphael's pyramidical Chigi monuments in Santa Maria del Popolo – to which Bernini had added portrait medallions – but organized and decorated the whole structure according to the principles of late seventeenth-century French architecture. The work was novel in that it comprised only two loosely connected parts, the coffin and the funeral obelisk. The apotheosis was no longer enacted before the eyes of the mourner, he was confronted with the monument of the deceased. The whole conception, in meaning as well as in architectural motifs and their arrangement, anticipates the principles of late eighteenth-century French neo-classical architecture.

This idea was continued in Fischer's design for the monument to the Chancellor of Bohemia, Graf Johann Wenzel Wratislaw von Mitrowitz, in St James's, Prague, executed in 1714. In this design for a permanent monument Fischer did not, however, venture so far from Baroque tradition. Here, too, the idea of immortal fame is symbolized by an ancient Egyptian pyramid, with Fame writing the inscription on it, but it is linked with the idea of the dead rising from the tomb and being borne off to eternity. Bernini's papal tombs and François Girardon's Richelieu monument (in the Sorbonne Church) were his models. Synthesizing motifs taken from Raphael, Bernini, and late seventeenth-century French architecture, Fischer created a type of monument that was later to be used by his son and other architects. These monuments, which can be traced back to Renaissance ideas, are stylistically in accordance with Fischer's 'classical' palace façades, designed at approximately the same time [76, 78, 81], which also had a decisive influence on later Baroque architecture in Austria.

As we have seen, Fischer's deep interest in the Palladian style was clearly reflected in the garden palaces and houses that he designed in the first few years following the turn of the century [66, 69, 70]. After his travels in north-west Europe in 1704 and his stay in Venice in 1707, however, the whole of his architecture seems to have undergone a transformation in this direction. His designs for a number of palace façades in Vienna were something quite new in the city. These façades consist, broadly speaking, of a central projection thrown into relief by a giant order embracing two storeys and surmounted by a triangular pediment, and of relatively unarticulated lateral sections. This arrangement of the elevation goes back ultimately to the Mannerist architecture of north Italy, to Palladio and his successors. In the seventeenth century the Palladian style of architecture was further developed in the Protestant countries of north and north-west Europe and in England especially, by blending it with elements of contemporary French architecture. Fischer's façades do not, however, produce the sober, 'rational' effect of the Palladian buildings of Protestant Europe, because their architectural details are taken from the Roman High Baroque and late seventeenth-century French architecture, and because their surfaces are so richly adorned with sculptural decoration. Moreover, the play of Baroque curves is still maintained in their portals, which support balconies, and in specially ornamented windows above – an architectural feature occupying the whole height of the fronts, and adding much to counterbalance the 'rational' effect of their basic structure.

The first of these palace façades which Fischer designed about 1708–9 was for the Chancellery of Bohemia [76] in the Wipplinger-strasse, opposite the Old Town Hall (Altes Rathaus) in Vienna. The original stimulus for this façade was certainly Chatsworth House in Derbyshire [77], but Fischer strengthened the French elements in the proportions of the storeys and even added Borro-minesque elements, especially in the concave recession of the central window. He also enlivened the relatively simple shape of the façade with richly sculptured decoration: the balcony with its allegorical statues and even the whole central projection appear to be borne by term figures; the coats of arms of Bohemia, Moravia, and Silesia decorate the windows; the emblem of Charles VI with the imperial eagle appears in the tympanum. Statues of the Bohemian kings adorn the balustrade of the attic – they are shown as precursors of the Emperor, to whose happy reign the inscription refers. The whole structure is crowned by the heraldic animal of Bohemia, the lion. The building was completed in 1714 and enlarged by Matthias Gerl after 1750.

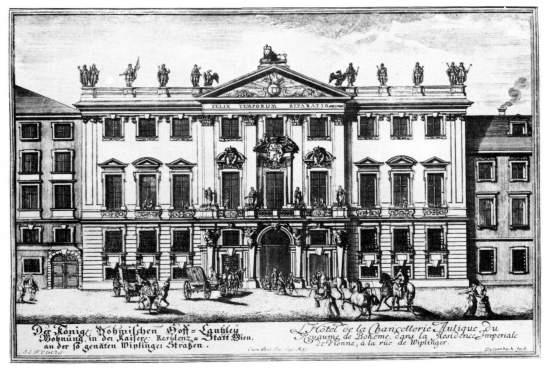

76. Chancellery of Bohemia, Vienna, façade

77. William Talman, Chatsworth House, west façade

Fischer adopted a similar approach in the façade of a palace at the city gates, built at approximately the same time for the influential Obersthofmeister (Lord High Steward) at the court of Emperor Joseph I, Johann Leopold Donat Graf Trautson (a prince of the Holy Roman Empire from 1711); it was probably designed in 1709 and begun in 1710. This 'residence' for the Lord High Steward –

78. Gartenpalais Trautson, Vienna, main façade

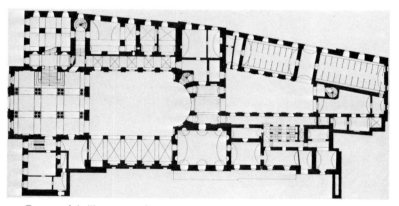

79. Gartenpalais Trautson, plan

opposite the Hofburg, the winter residence of the Emperor – was a new type of building in Vienna: a great town palace with a garden outside the city walls. The main façade [78], facing the Hofburg and the city, is different from that of the Bohemian Chancellery [76] in that the central part projects far more (there was more room on this site than in the narrow streets of the city),

80. Gartenpalais Trautson, staircase

and in the use of a curved motif for the portal – two double columns mounted on high, obliquely placed pedestals with a slightly curved entablature. This whole structure seems to be placed in front of the façade like a piece of stage scenery. Fischer has found here the most 'classical' solution to the problem presented by this new type of façade in the harmony of proportions. The organization of the main façade is repeated with rather less decoration in the extended garden façade joining it at right angles, and in the first section of the otherwise undecorated façade on the suburban side-street. The calm, monumental effect of the main façade is echoed in the almost square and practically unadorned entrance hall of nine bays dominated by four groups of four Tuscan columns [79], as well as in the imposing staircase supported by atlantes and guarded by sphinxes [80]. This staircase takes up the full height of the side section on the left and, although it is as sober as the staircase in the Palais Batthyány [49], it also contains High Baroque elements reminiscent of Prince Eugene's Town Palace [46]. Originally there were two courtyards behind the entrance hall; the first, opening immediately behind it, was oblong and had an apsidal rear wall (like Antoine Le Pautre's Hôtel Beauvais in Paris). Thus, from the entrance door there was a fine vista through the whole complex of buildings. Both courts were decorated in a restrained, almost chaste manner recalling French architecture. (The courts were recently demolished and replaced by an office building for the Ministry of Justice, screened by the still extant garden façade, which was restored at the same time as the main façade, entrance hall and staircase.)

The iconographical programme for the decoration of the building can be but partially reconstructed, as so much has been destroyed. The decorative sculpture on the main façade celebrated the glory of Prince Trautson – the reliefs above the windows, figures of gods on the attic, and a whole Olympus in the tympanum alluded to his virtues and achievements. Apollo playing the lyre – the symbol of a nobleman who is a patron of science and the arts – stands on the apex of the pediment. The apotheosis of the person for whom the house was built appearing on the main façade of the palace was something quite new – previously, it had always appeared on the ceiling of the principal room.

At the side (not at the rear, as was usual) of this 'classical' palace there was a French garden with some Roman High Baroque elements. The garden wall with its oval windows was very similar to that surrounding the garden of the Villa Aldobrandini at Frascati, designed by Bizzaccheri. The orangery was basically a resumption of Fischer's park gate designs for the Liechtenstein Palace [2, 3] and the stables of the Bergschloss [57]. Here, however, Fischer's favourite belvedere motif was stripped of its dynamism under the influence of his new style. (The garden was destroyed in the second half of the eighteenth century; but now there are plans to lay out a park on its site.)

Fischer also used this new type of façade in Prague. The town palace belonging to Johann Wenzel Graf Gallas in the Altstadt (Staré Město) [81] was rebuilt according to his design from 1713 onwards. (Graf Gallas, who had been Marshal of Bohemia since 1708, had been sent as imperial envoy first to London, then to the Papal court, and was Viceroy of Naples when he died in 1719.) Though Fischer was hampered by the awkward site, a rather irregular, medieval complex of buildings with a high tower facing

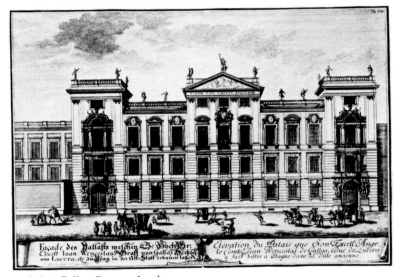

81. Palais Gallas, Prague, façade

82. Serlio, palace façade

a narrow street, he turned it to advantage. The need to incorporate the medieval tower and his growing tendency to build higher façades resulted here in a front accented by three tower-like projections. This façade is a synthesis of three types of façade in the Palladian tradition. The three tower-like projections are an idea of Serlio's [82]; the central part derives from late seventeenth-century English architecture; and the two side projections with their combinations of portal and window above, here embracing three storeys, follow Andreas Schlüter's design for the central section of the garden façade of the Royal Palace in Berlin [83]. As in the other façades of this group, Fischer inserted Borrominesque details (windows, doors, balconies) and enlivened it further with *mouve-*

83. Andreas Schlüter, Royal Palace, Berlin, garden façade

84. Palais Gallas, Prague, entrance

menté Berninesque sculpture [84]. Though the projections are relatively slight, the façade is one of Fischer's most monumental achievements. Its outstanding aspects are the dynamic roof-line and the tower-like side projections with their massive portals crowned by large windows, which accentuate the vertical tendency of these bays, making them look more slender and soaring because of the apparent elimination of the walls. The iconographical programme of the main façade comprises the deeds of Hercules and Apollo (represented by the statues of the portals), heroic scenes of gods and heroes alluding to the virtues of a nobleman (in the reliefs above the windows), and an Olympus in the pediment. The statues of the gods on the attic are dominated by a figure of Jupiter at the apex of the pediment. The inscription also contributes to this apotheosis of Graf Gallas.

Fischer used this 'Palladian' type of façade in 1710 for a much smaller structure – the central pavilion of the villa in the Wienerwald, commissioned by the envoy of the Electorate of Hanover at the Viennese court, Daniel Erasmus von Huldenberg. This small garden palace at Weidlingau, which was characteristically the only one on the outskirts of Vienna to be called a 'villa', was a completely new type of building for Vienna and one which incidentally aroused the interest of the Swedish architect and collector Nikodemus Tessin the Younger. It was completed in 1715; a ruin since the Second World War, it was recently demolished. The 'Palladian' type of façade also forms the basis of Fischer's design for the great hall of Stift Herzogenburg in Lower Austria (1716).

This type of palace façade, with its tension between Palladian and Roman High Baroque elements, proved to be extremely fruitful in Austrian architecture and also spread into the other countries of the Habsburg Empire. Fischer's portals for this group of palaces were used, with variations, in a number of later palaces in Vienna and were also imitated in Prague.

g. *Imperial Architecture*

The grandiose residence which Fischer had designed at the beginning of his period of activity at the Viennese court [9] was, to his great sorrow, never built. Towards the end of his life, however, he was offered two commissions of comparable dimensions by the Emperor Charles VI – the Karlskirche, and the rebuilding of the Hofburg. Fischer did not live to see his two great projects completed. At least one year before his death he was prevented by a severe illness from visiting the building sites and supervising the construction. His son continued his work, although he made certain changes. Especially in the case of the Karlskirche, it is not at all easy to decide which changes were introduced by the son, because the father had been responsible for some changes himself during the long period of building.

To deliver Vienna from an epidemic of the plague which raged in the city in 1713, the Emperor Charles VI vowed to build a church dedicated to St Charles Borromeo. All the Habsburg dominions were to contribute to the cost of the building, in accordance with the 'pragmatic sanction' in which the Emperor had declared, that same year, that all the hereditary Habsburg countries were indivisible and inseparable and that his daughters would succeed to them in the event of extinction in the male line. A competition was held for the design of the church and towards the end of 1715 the Emperor accepted Fischer's plan. The foundation stone was laid on 4 February 1716. Fischer's first designs have been preserved in the plates in his history of architecture [85, 91, 92] and it is remarkable in how many ways the building itself differs from them [90, 95]. By the end of 1720, 300 oak trees had been ordered for the roof so that the dome could be vaulted the following year. In 1721 the columns for the drum of the dome were fashioned. At the beginning of 1722, when Fischer's son returned to Vienna, his father was hardly capable of directing the work any longer. On 24 March 1723 the Emperor commanded Fischer the younger to continue with the supervision of the building. We may conclude from these dates that changes in the designs for the drum and the dome were already made during Johann Bernhard Fischer's lifetime and obviously with his sanction. It has so far not been possible to establish with certainty the extent to which the father and the son contributed towards these changes. The drum and the dome itself were completed in 1725 and the interior decoration was finished, in accordance with the programme of Conrad Adolph von Albrecht, in 1738. In the same year the church was handed over to an order of chivalry – the Kreuzherrenorden mit dem roten Stern – in the presence of the Emperor.

The Karlskirche [85], built outside the city proper on a mound on the bank of the river Wien and originally facing the imperial palace, has a façade unlike any other Baroque church. The complex formal and symbolic structure is the result of its twofold function – as a votive church and as a monument to the greatness of a dynasty. In conformity with the Emperor's vow, it is dedicated to St Charles Borromeo, who was one of the saints whose intercession was invoked during the plague and who was also the name saint of the Emperor. The spiral reliefs on the two columns represent – by analogy with Trajan's column in Rome – scenes from St Charles Borromeo's life and the miracles he performed after his death. Statues symbolizing the saint's virtues stand on the attic between

Prospect der Neuen Kirchen S. Caroli Borromæi,
welche Seine Kayserlich- und Catholische Majestät, Unser-
allergnädigster Herr Herr Carl der Sechste, als ein gelübd
erbauen lasset in Wienn, unweit der Favoriten,
Cum Privil. Sac: Cæsar Maiest.

Vuë de la nouvelle Eglise de S. Charles Borromé, que Sa
Majesté Imperiale et Catholique, Nôtre très auguste
Monarque et Seigneur Charles VI fait bâtir, en ayant
fait væu, à Vienne, pas loin de la Favorite

85. Karlskirche, Vienna, project for front

the columns. One of his deeds, the deliverance of Vienna from the
plague, forms the subject of the relief on the tympanum of the
porch. The statue above, at the apex of the pediment over the main
entrance, shows the saint in the attitude of an intercessor for
mankind and thus embodies one of the three theological virtues –
charity. The other two virtues – faith and hope – are represented
by allegorical statues surmounting the towers. The saint's apotheosis is symbolized by the soaring outline of the dome. On the
exterior the dome is guarded by statues of angels; inside, a fresco
depicting the glory of the saint, surrounded by angels in adoration
of the Holy Trinity, seems to open up a vision of heaven (though
this fresco, painted after Fischer's death, was not part of the
original project).

In the image of his name saint, however, the Emperor himself
was glorified by this church. The pair of triumphal columns was
his own emblem, which he had taken over from his ancestor and
predecessor as Holy Roman Emperor and King of Spain, Charles V.

These 'pillars of Hercules' therefore bear the crown of Spain at their summits, flanked by eagles, the heraldic beast of the Holy Roman Empire. The deeds of St Charles represented on the columns allude simultaneously to the *constantia et fortitudo* of Charles VI (his motto), qualities which helped him to endure every turn of fortune. The dynastic significance of the columns is

86. Martin van Heemskerck, Temple of Jerusalem

87. Temple of Concordia in Forum Romanum, illustration on a coin

88. Bernini, project for façade of St Peter's

made clearer if we bear in mind that the philosopher Leibniz had suggested that saintly ancestors and 'namesakes' of the Emperor – Charlemagne and Charles of Flanders – should also be glorified in the Karlskirche, and that the imperial antiquary Heraeus wanted their deeds to be represented in the reliefs on the columns. Had this intention been carried out it would have provided another allusion to the achievements of the dynasty for the Empire and, in particular, to the southern Netherlands, which had been won back by Charles VI.

The Karlskirche stands at the end of a long line of sacred buildings and represents the architect's attempt to incorporate and harmonize the main ideas contained in the most important of them. Fischer had reconstructed some of these buildings in his history of architecture shortly before [106, 108]. The determining prototype from the visual and iconographical points of view seems to have been the Temple in Jerusalem, which architects of the time supposed to be the basis of all sacred buildings in Europe. In Mannerist prints it had been represented, in accordance with I Kings vii, 13–22, as a domed building with a porch flanked by two huge columns (c.f. Philipp Galle's engraving after a drawing by Martin van Heemskerck [86]). The statues of Ecclesia and Synagogue are consequently placed beside the giant columns, on either side of the steps leading to the entrance of the Karlskirche. Reminiscences of the Pantheon in Rome, with its columnar portico, the façade of the Temple of Concordia in the Forum Romanum [87], of Hagia Sophia in Constantinople, with the minarets surrounding it, and, of course, of St Peter's in Rome, cannot be overlooked [88]. Fischer was also influenced by the most important seventeenth-century French churches – especially François Mansart's Église des Minimes [89] but also the Dôme des Invalides

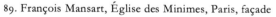

89. François Mansart, Église des Minimes, Paris, façade

(which was in iconography also closely related to its founder, Louis XIV). Finally, the Karlskirche reflects ideas from Wren's design for St Paul's Cathedral. (Whether Fischer knew Juvarra's early projects for the Superga outside Turin is not yet clear.) Fischer's 'summa' of religious architecture was conceived as a glorification of the Emperor: he was extolled as a second Solomon and as a second Augustus initiating a period of peace, and as a legitimate successor to the Roman Emperors. Like Constantinople in the past, Vienna was now the 'new Rome'. These interpretations taken from the literature of the time reveal that the complicated iconographical programme was fully understood by Fischer's contemporaries.

The individual parts of the front of the church – the dome, the two columns, side-towers and portico – are attuned with one another by their proportions and bound together by dynamic tension. Apart from the synthesis of the main architectural styles of the seventeenth century, characteristic of Fischer's work in general, the prominent use of antique architectural elements is the most striking feature of the Karlskirche. This testifies to the increasing influence of the Palladian tradition and to Fischer's deep involvement in archaeological research. In accordance with the principles of late seventeenth-century French architecture, particularly as expounded by François Blondel, the relatively independent parts of the building are harmonized to form a visual unity. (In the course of designing and constructing the church French tendencies towards unification increased.) As a result, there is no façade in the usual sense but rather a frontal view [90] and a composite structural group with several different aspects [93, 94], consisting of heterogeneous elements, but unified by the recurrence of certain motifs both on the exterior and interior of the building. But the deepest impression is made only on those who are able to comprehend both the form and content of the church when looking at it. From a distance, the front facing the imperial palace appears, in the harmony of its proportions, as a self-contained 'picture'. Just as Fischer's first Schönbrunn project [9] represented the ideal residence as a monument to Roman imperial power, the Karlskirche is the ideal church as a monument to dynastic greatness. In its spiritual conception it has no predecessor, and in the uniqueness of its realization it has no successor.

The engraving of the front of the Karlskirche in Fischer's history of architecture [85] is an ideal view probably based on the first design that was submitted to the Emperor. It was above all a visual conception and it seems as though it became necessary to modify this first design when the ground-plan was prepared [91]. The interior is basically an oval, the longitudinal axis of which is

90. Karlskirche, front

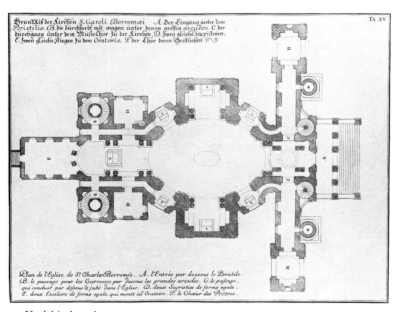

91. Karlskirche, plan

directed towards the altar. It is surmounted by a dome above a very high drum and has barrel-vaulted transepts. Around the central space on the diagonal axes there are oval side-chapels with galleries [92]. Fischer had already employed this basic idea in the

92. Karlskirche, section

ground plan of his Dreifaltigkeitskirche in Salzburg [20]. The immediate models for the ground-plan of the Karlskirche are, however, to be found in seventeenth-century French architecture and, in particular, in Louis Le Vau's Collège des Quatre Nations in Paris (1660/63–8), in which, besides other similarities of plan and elevation (e.g. the arrangement of niches and galleries above in the piers supporting the main dome), a choir dome is also placed behind the main dome. Fischer's idea of connecting the presbytery with the priests' choir behind it by means of a columnar screen goes back to Palladio's Venetian churches.

Compared with the first designs, the building itself, viewed from the outside [90], seems more slender in its proportions and more harmonious as a whole. The side towers are connected by an attic, which screens the lower part of the drum of the dome, so that its convex projection does not contrast too strongly with the flat temple portico. The drum itself is not evenly surrounded by pairs of columns, as Fischer had originally planned [85]; its relief is flatter, but its diagonal axes are accentuated. In this way, its cylindrical form is less strongly emphasized. The more slender and delicate shape of the lantern surmounting the dome is undoubtedly also in accordance with this tendency. Seen as a whole, the building

93. Karlskirche, rear view

94. Karlskirche, side view

marks a departure from the eminently sculptural, dynamic combination of elements discernible in Fischer's first design and a decision to increase the harmony of the structure instead. In the interior, too, the diagonal axes are given much greater emphasis than they were in the original design. The priests' choir behind the presbytery was not executed; the presbytery was closed off by a straight wall instead. As in the University Church in Salzburg [30] there is no special structure for the high altar, but the whole wall, framed by columns, is taken up with a stucco decoration showing the glory of St Charles Borromeo, the sign of Yahweh in a halo hovering above [95]. Instead of being decorated with coffers like the Roman Pantheon, as was originally planned, the dome was given a fresco

95. Karlskirche, interior

showing the apotheosis of the patron saint of the church [96]. The
very high interior of the building makes its greatest impact on the
visitor through the monumental quality of its structural forms and
the cool harmony of its colours – in the Baroque period, red-brown,
white, and gold signified dignity and stately appearance. The
architectural details must to a very great extent have been worked
out by Fischer's son, Joseph Emanuel.

At about the same time as he was working on his first designs
for the Karlskirche, Fischer was designing a chapel in which he

97. Wrocław (Breslau) Cathedral, Elector's Chapel, interior

reduced the interior of the Viennese church but combined, in a highly individual manner, Palladian and Borrominian ideas. The Bishop of Breslau and Worms, Franz Ludwig von Neuburg, an uncle of the Emperor and later the Elector of Trier and finally of Mainz, gave him a commission to design his mausoleum, the Elector's Chapel, next to the choir of the Cathedral of Breslau (now Wrocław). The chapel was built between 1715 or 1716 and 1721 and was dedicated in 1724. The ground-plan and structure of the interior follow those of the chapel's counterpart on the opposite side of the choir, which was influenced by Borromini. The relatively small space [97] is in many respects reminiscent of Borromini's San Carlo alle Quattro Fontane in Rome. But Fischer rejected in principle Borromini's 'undulating' ground-plans in favour of the pure oval. The interior of the chapel is characterized by the diversity of architectonic forms in the four vertical zones and by the rich variation of plans in the horizontal. The rectangular space is covered by an oval dome, its longitudinal axis in line with that of the church. The central section of the side walls follows the curve of the dome. This results in the entablature being bent in a complicated manner, very sharply outlined and in striking contrast to the pure oval of the cupola. The round, domed altar space with its demi-circle of columns – to some extent a combination of Palladian and Borrominesque ideas – is joined to the main space by the entablature, yet separated from it by a kind of triumphal arch, a slender barrel-vault supported on two columns. These features mark the main difference between the architecture of Fischer and Borromini: in Fischer's buildings the spatial elements are independent parts of the whole, in Borromini's they are merged into one, hence the undulating lines of his ground-plans. In the Elector's Chapel the main emphasis is laid on the interior and the exterior is comparatively sparsely decorated. The programme of the interior decoration expresses the chapel's function as a mausoleum dedicated to the Eucharist. This chapel occupies a special place in Fischer's architecture, for here he came closer to Borromini's ideas than in any other work. He also made use of details, such as the Borrominesque seraphim-headed terms on the drum of the dome, which occur nowhere else in his *œuvre*.

The Karlskirche was conceived with its main front facing the Hofburg; this connection can no longer be observed because of the building of the Ringstrasse in the nineteenth century. Indeed, at the time of the architectural competition for the church, Charles VI intended to have the Imperial Palace transformed into a grandiose residence. As early as 1716 plans were made, undoubtedly by Fischer, for a new building for the imperial library, as well as a design, nothing of which has come down to us, for an imperial academy of sciences. It was in about 1719 that Fischer began to build the huge Hofstallungen – imperial stables – outside the city walls opposite the part of the Imperial Palace erected by Leopold I, and it is clear that a total concept for the extension of the imperial residence must have already existed at this time. Although no evidence survives, there can be little doubt that Fischer was the author of this plan, which must have been in no way inferior in grandeur to his first project for Schönbrunn [9]. It is also probable that the younger Fischer, Joseph Emanuel, based his plans for the Imperial Palace on ideas which originated in his father's mind. The great semicircle of the palace courtyard on the Michaelerplatz, which was begun by Joseph Emanuel and only completed, in accordance with his plans, in the nineteenth century, may well contain a last echo of Johann Bernhard Fischer's original idea.

The gigantic complex of the Hofstallungen [98], built to house 600 horses, is spread out opposite the Imperial Palace and at a seemly distance from it, and was intended to provide an element of 'magnificence' in the view from the palace. Fischer conceived the

98. Project for Hofstallungen (imperial stables), Vienna

Prospect des Großen Neuen Kayst: Stalls vor 600 Pferde, welcher anjezo im bau begriffen ist. A. der große Hoff ein Carrousel dar: inn zuhalten. B. amphiteatrum vor die Zuschauer, ünter desi: en arcaden, die wagen Schupffen sind. C. die Pferdt Schwemme. D. die vorstadt Leimgruben. E. vorstadt St. Ulrich.

Fischers Del.

Vue du grand Bâtiment nouveau des Ecuries Imperiales, pour 600 chevaux, que l'on bâtit actuellement. A. la grande Cour pour le Carrousel. B. L'Amphiteatre pour les Spectateurs, sous les Arcades duquel sont les remises de Carosses. C. L'abbreuvoir des chevaux. D. le Fauxbourg nommé Leimgruben. E. Faubourg St. Ulric.

Cum Priv. Sac. Cæs. Maj.

stables in reminiscence of his reconstructions of vast buildings from the Roman imperial era, especially Nero's Domus Aurea, from which he took the semicircular court with a basin, flanked by extended lateral ranges, and Diocletian's Thermae – which accounts for his idea of shaping the semicircle as an amphitheatre. Bramante had already partly revived such vast buildings of ancient Rome in his designs for the Belvedere courtyard of the Vatican Palace, in which there is also a semicircular amphitheatre with lateral pavilions intended for carousels. Though only a part of Bramante's project was executed Fischer was undoubtedly acquainted with it. The extended façade of Fischer's imperial stables consists of a series of almost independent structural elements and is, in this respect, very similar to the Neo-Palladian architecture appearing in north Germany at approximately the same time. The central pavilion, the quarters of the master of the Emperor's horses, is distinguished by Fischer's 'Palladian' type of façade [see 76, 78]. Only the central pavilion and the two lateral pavilions project from the front of the building as a whole – the remaining sections, the stables themselves, are relatively narrow and slightly articulated. Despite its great length, the whole façade does not make a monotonous impression in Fischer's design. It is given a certain rhythm by the outline of the roof, the dynamic flow of which culminates in the centre. Moreover, the corner pavilions are accentuated by pediments and towers which are reminiscent of belvederes. Behind the main entrance there is a three-aisled passage from which it is possible to reach the pavilions at each side of the central pavilion. In each of these there is an oval-shaped room, probably used as a riding school, with the ceiling resting on four supports (another Palladian idea). It is only outside this main building, consisting of three pavilions, that the stables proper begin. These take the form of long corridors, interrupted only by the side passages. On the upper storey of the stable buildings were the quarters for the staff. The long front range was completed in 1723 by the younger Fischer, but the section at the rear was not built until the nineteenth century, following Fischer's structural design. The imperial stables, which have, of course, been somewhat altered both inside and out, are used nowadays as an exhibition building for the Viennese Trade Fair.

In 1681 the foundations for a riding school had been laid between the medieval part of the Hofburg and the Augustinian monastery. The Emperor Leopold I had begun to build this riding school with the intention of housing his library on the upper storey, but the work was brought to a standstill by the Turkish siege of the city. Fischer had submitted new plans for the imperial library in 1716 – plans known to Leibniz – but it was not until 1722 that sufficient money was available for the project to be carried out. The library was eventually built, in accordance with Fischer's plans, by his son between 1723 and 1726. The interior decoration was not completed, however, until 1737 and we must assume that Joseph Emanuel had a considerable share in its design. At the beginning of the work of construction, substructures were fastened to the existing foundations of the riding school with iron bolts, to support the oval-shaped central hall of the library which projected on both façades. But this precaution proved inadequate, because the southern projection subsided only forty years later, causing damage to the building and threatening the dome. Maria Theresa's court architect, Nikolaus Pacassi, had to put up walls in the cellar, insert pillars in the central hall and stretch two arches between them to support the dome. He also built the wings on either side of the court according to his own design.

Just as Fischer had turned to exemplars when designing his other exceptional commissions – Schloss Schönbrunn and the Karlskirche – so he looked now to the great library buildings of the past and present, considering their form as well as their symbolism, in order to find the ideal solution to his problem. The foundations for the riding school which had already been laid obliged him to build on a long, extended ground-plan. He therefore based his project on an oblong hall with barrel-vaulting [100, 101, 102], similar to the library of the Escorial which, when it was built towards the end of the sixteenth century, had been the first great library to have open bookshelves. Fischer combined this Mannerist type of library with an oval domed hall in such a way that the longitudinal axes of the two spaces intersected in the centre [100, 101, 104]. The idea of a centrally planned library had, on the advice of Leibniz, already been realized a few years previously by Hermann Korb at Wolfenbüttel. This first ovally planned and free-standing library building (with a passage around it at ground level and galleries above), bore as a visible sign of its scientific function a gigantic celestial globe on its high roof. Other features of Fischer's library were taken from Borromini. The idea of a library hall several storeys high, its walls entirely covered by bookshelves on which elaborately bound volumes are displayed, and horizontally divided by a gallery resting on consoles, is reminiscent of Borromini's Biblioteca Alessandrina in Rome. The stair turrets, the gallery supported by slender wooden piers, and the richly decorated superstructures above the bookshelves in the central hall recall another interior by Borromini, the library of the Oratorio di San Filippo Neri, Rome.

This synthesis of the most important types of library interior of the time is harmonized on the exterior by combining the French pavilion system with Palladian and High Baroque elements. The three projections are accentuated by big portals and high central windows above, by monumental groups of sculpture on their attics, and by high mansard roofs. The middle projection is rather prominent, but its convex shape is screened by a straight wall. The practice of screening a semicircle by a polygonal structure derives from mid-seventeenth-century French architecture (e.g. Jean Marot's Château de Turny). Fischer, however, allowed parts of the basic oval shape to be seen on the outside. The lightly battered ground storey decorated with horizontal grooves, into which simple portals are cut like niches, is also derived from French architecture. It is possible that the sober structure of this lower

99. Hofbibliothek (imperial library), Vienna, north façade

Facies nova Bibliothecæ Cæsareæ incomparabilis .   Prospect der neüerbauten Kayserlichen unvergleichlichen Bibliothec.

storey reflects its function, for it served as a coach house and was not equipped as a bookstore until the present century.

Above this massive substructure, the great hall of the library itself rises, occupying the whole length of the building. The long barrel-vaulted gallery [100, 101] is divided by the oval central hall into two wings, which are in turn subdivided by arrangements of columns. Fischer's use of the Palladian motif of a columnar screen in a barrel-vaulted hall is strikingly reminiscent of Antonio del Grande's gallery of 1665 in the Palazzo Colonna in Rome [103]. Viewed from the entrance [102], these columns make the library look longer and wider. Seen from the central hall [104], which communicates with the wings by means of the high arches supporting the dome, the columns mark off the central part of the library from the entrance and in this way serve to emphasize the tendency towards centralization.

The plan of the building – a central oval surmounted by a dome and flanked by wings – reveals its inner meaning in the programme for the interior and exterior decoration. This was conceived by Conrad Adolph von Albrecht even before the construction of the library was begun, in other words, at approximately the same time as Fischer's designs. It has been preserved in two manuscripts

100. Hofbibliothek (imperial library), plan of main floor

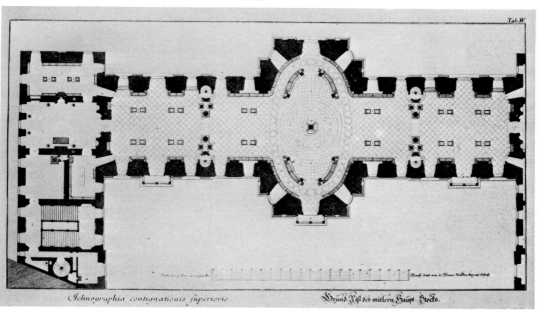

101. Hofbibliothek (imperial library), section

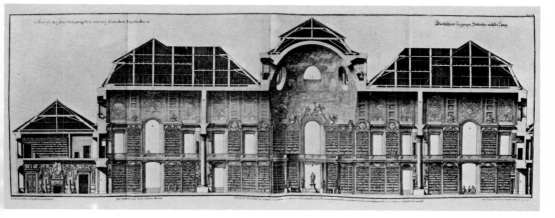

102. Hofbibliothek (imperial library), Vienna, axial view

103. Antonio del Grande, gallery of Palazzo Colonna, Rome

104. Hofbibliothek (imperial library), central oval hall

(Vienna, Österreichische Nationalbibliothek, Cod. 8334 and 7853). Explanations of the sculptured and painted decorations are also inscribed on a series of engravings of the library published by Salomon Kleiner in 1737 [100, 101]. Fischer combined Leibniz's idea of the ideal library as a temple of books with the idea of a temple of fame which he had already realized in a similar way, but on a smaller scale, at Schloss Frain [4]. The two wings are subordinated to this central hall; the one next to the Imperial Palace embodies the sciences of peace, the other the sciences of war. It was the Emperor who protected and promoted both of them, and his emblem, the pillars of Hercules, supports the vaults of the wings. A statue of the Emperor, surrounded by statues of his ancestors, transforms the central oval of the library into an ancestral hall, while the dome above glorifies in its paintings both the Emperor as the lord of war and peace and the whole house of Habsburg. Allegorical allusions are made in these ceiling frescoes to the wars Charles VI waged against the Turks, to the War of the Spanish Succession and to the successful part he played as a patron of the arts and sciences. The inscription below his portrait in the centre of this whole configuration calls him a hero of war and of peace, a 'Hercules of the Muses'. The idea of this entire iconographical programme and its execution, in the ceiling paintings of Daniel Gran, were enthusiastically praised by Johann Joachim Winckelmann as a model of allegorical art. The imperial library in Vienna is more than a palace of books. In form as well as in significance – by glorifying the Emperor and the dynasty, the lords of war and peace and patrons of art and science – it is almost a sacred building.

The staircase to the hall of the library was originally situated in the left wing [100]. After passing an adjoining room, the 'antecamera' immediately in front of the great hall was reached [101, left]. The antiquarian character of this anteroom is clearly revealed by the ancient remains let into the walls, the broken-off columns on pedestals made in imitation of natural rock, and the fireplaces copying ancient monuments in ruins. To what extent the idea for this interior was the elder Fischer's is not certain, but the elements contained in it are certainly exemplified in his work. Later, during the reign of Maria Theresa, this anteroom was transformed by Nikolaus Pacassi and converted into a staircase, but the upper part, with the ancient milestones, votive altars and sepulchral monuments set into the wall, is still preserved. It reflects the antiquarian interests of the imperial court and the lively connection between architecture and archaeology of the period.

Most of Fischer's works were 'historical' buildings. From the very beginning his attitude towards architecture was retrospective. He looked back at the great architectural achievements of the past with the aim of synthetically forming something new, his own works, out of them. He took as his sources both the ancient style of building and the modern styles since the Renaissance, in which the ancient style had been given new life. He regarded a knowledge of the great buildings of the past as indispensable to modern architects, for whom his history of architecture was intended. The seed which grew into this work was undoubtedly sown in Rome, when Fischer met a number of archaeologists and antiquaries, notably Athanasius Kircher and Giovanni Pietro Bellori. The idea may also have been encouraged by his activity as tutor in architecture to Joseph I. The immediate incentive, however, was probably a meeting with Sir Christopher Wren in London, who was preoccupied with very similar ideas. It was in London too that Fischer must have come across descriptions of journeys in the East, volumes which also contained sketches and reconstructions of ruins. He began work on his return from England in 1705 and dedicated the manuscript of his *Entwurff Einer Historischen Architectur*, with the proofs of seventy-four plates, mostly engravings by J. A. Delsenbach, to Emperor Charles VI in 1712. The first edition, with ninety plates and a text in German and French, appeared in 1721 in Vienna. This edition comprised only 160 copies. A second edition appeared in 1725 in Leipzig and this was reprinted in 1742. In 1730 a reprint of the 1725 edition appeared in large octavo format, translated into English by Thomas Lediard and entitled *A Plan of Civil and Historical Architecture*. A second impression appeared in 1737.

Fischer and the architects of his time believed that Roman architecture went back to the orders of the Temple of Solomon, where these orders had been used for the first time. For this reason Nicolai Goldmann had placed this temple as the most perfect building, above his own designs, in his textbook of civil architecture, published by Leonhard Christian Sturm in 1696; Carlo Fontana had arranged his history of St Peter's, Rome, of 1694 in a similar way. What was new in Fischer's work was that, taking the Temple of Solomon as his point of departure, he consistently traced the whole development of architecture, including that of non-European civilizations, and exemplified it in different types of buildings. In his first book he showed, besides the Temple of Solomon, the seven wonders of the world [e.g. 105] and the buildings of ancient Egypt, Persia and Greece, while the second book is devoted to Roman architecture [106, 107]. To judge from the title of the

105. Reconstruction of Babylon, including Tower of Babel

manuscript, this book should originally have included Gothic and
'Moorish' buildings. The third book is devoted to the architecture
of Islam, medieval and modern Persia, and China [108, 109]; the
fourth contains Fischer's own works, which he, like architects
generally since the Renaissance, regarded as the natural continuation
of Roman architecture. In this fourth part of his history of architecture Fischer classified his own designs and buildings first
according to type and second, within these groups, according to
the social rank of the person from whom he received the commission [72, 9, 65, 42, 81, 24, 85, 92, 91, 98, 66, 53, 69, 58]. In the
fifth book, once again taking the same point of departure – the
Temple of Solomon with its sea of molten bronze (1 Kings vii,
23ff.) – and following the same sequence, he showed various
designs of vases – Egyptian, Greek, Roman, and his own – combined with a building in a corresponding style in the background
[57, 1, 2]. In this work of Fischer's the idea of a comparative history
of architecture covering all periods and all civilizations is realized
for the first time. In tracing the Corinthian order back to the Temple
of Solomon, Fischer gave his work a religious motivation.

His manner of reconstructing ancient buildings is very striking
and shows that he was fully acquainted with the findings of contemporary archaeology. Stimulated by the work of the Roman

106. Reconstruction of Trajan's Forum

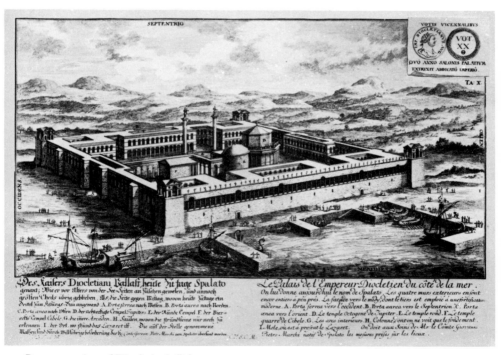

107. Reconstruction of Diocletian's Palace

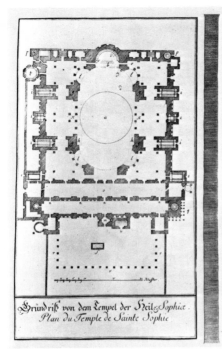

TA. VI.

Grundriß von dem Tempel der Heil. Sophiæ
Plan du Temple de Sainte Sophie

Der berühmte Tempel St. Sophiæ
in Constantinopol nahe bey dem Serais

Le grand et magnifique temple
de Sainte Sophie proche du Serail

108. Hagia Sophia, view and plan

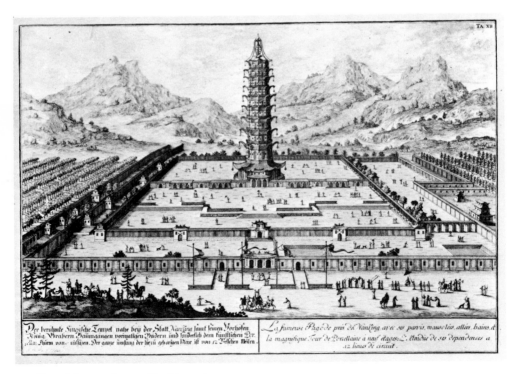

TA. XII

Der berühmte Sinesische Tempel nahe bey der Statt Nanquin samt seinen Vorhofen Königl. Grabern Baumgangen vormaligen Badern und sonderlich dem künstlichen Porcellan Thurm von . . . aussehen. Der gantze innhalt der hierzu gehörigen Platz ist von 12 Welschen Meilen.

La fameuse Pagôde près de Nanking avec ses parvis, mausolées, allées, bains et la magnifique Tour de Porcellaine a neuf étages étendue de ses dependences a 12 lieues de circuit.

109. Porcelain pagoda near Nanking, view

archaeologist Bellori and of the two antiquaries Jacques Spon and George Wheler (*Voyage d'Italie, de Dalmatie, de Grèce et du Levant*, first published in Lyons in 1678), he consulted written sources (ancient authors and modern descriptions of journeys – these sources are indicated in connection with every plate in his book), coins and those ruins which were still standing. Wherever possible, he tried to procure drawings of the buildings or ruins and this also helped him to achieve, at least in certain cases, remarkably correct results [e.g. 107]. In this, he was the forerunner of the archaeologists who published great works in the second half of the eighteenth century and who frequently used his plates in their own books.

Despite all his serious attempts to be archaeologically accurate – a task in which he was greatly helped by his friend Heraeus, the numismatologist and antiquarian, who was also the author of the texts accompanying the plates – Fischer was still a Baroque architect. Whenever his sources provided him with insufficient or no information he did not hesitate to use his artistic imagination. Combining details which he had correctly reconstructed on the basis of archaeological research, he designed typically Baroque prospects [105, 106]. He saw his own works as marking the end of a long process of development which had begun with the Temple of Jerusalem. As they included ideas derived from historical buildings, Fischer also equipped the historical buildings in his book with elements of modern architecture. A few examples may help to illustrate the different points of view that are present in his reconstructions.

Attempts to reconstruct the Tower of Babel, which had already been depicted in the Middle Ages, had been made with the help of descriptions by Herodotus, Strabo and Pliny since the sixteenth century. By scrupulously following Strabo's description Fischer broke with the 200-year-old tradition of rendering the building as a round tower tapering towards the top and surrounded by spiral ramps, and reconstructed it, almost correctly, as a step pyramid [105]. Fischer was, however, far less interested in the Tower than in the 'hanging gardens' of Babylon. In designing them he made use of the view of Babylon published in Athanasius Kircher's archaeological work *Turris Babel* (Amsterdam, 1679). In many details Fischer was closer to the ancient authors than Kircher, even though he represented the gardens as a monumental French park with several parterres arranged in terraces.

Fischer based his completely individual representation of Trajan's Roman Forum [106] mainly on two works about Trajan's column – the first written by Alfonso Ciacconi and published by Bellori (*Colonna Traiana*, Rome, 1650) and the second by Raffaele Fabretti (*Columna Traiani Syntagma*, Rome, 1683) – in which the buildings of the Forum were reconstructed from illustrations on Roman coins. In his version, however, Fischer consciously disregarded the historical data and produced something quite distinctive. The equestrian statues of the Emperors Trajan and Marcus Aurelius, the fountain, the symmetrical arrangement of the square with the column in the centre and the uniformity of the surrounding buildings clearly go back to the classical French idea of the 'Place Royale' (see, for example, Jules-Hardouin Mansart's Place des Victoires and Place Vendôme in Paris, 1685 and 1686 respectively).

For his reconstruction of Diocletian's Palace [107], Fischer drew on the archaeological descriptions by Spon and Wheler, but was also able to make use of contemporary drawings of the ruins, which were sent to him directly from Spalato. The result was the first reconstruction of the building which was really faithful to the archaeological data.

Fischer included the church of Hagia Sophia in Constantinople [108] among the Turkish architectural monuments and did not reconstruct the Byzantine church, but presented it with the four minarets added by the Turks. (It was in this form that the building influenced the design of the Karlskirche.) His main source here was G. J. Grelot's *Relation nouvelle d'un voyage de Constantinople*, published in Paris in 1680.

He used Jean Nieuhoff's account of a journey made by a Dutch legation to the Emperor of China (Leiden, 1655) for his reconstruction of the porcelain pagoda at Nanking [109]. Responding to the current vogue for China, Fischer had himself designed two 'Chinese rooms', one in Schönbrunn Palace and the other in the Hofburg. But in his case, this fashion led to no more than the faithful imitation of outlandish forms. He never engaged in the wilful transformation of Chinese motifs in the French Rococo manner.

In the ancient Egyptian section Fischer placed a view of the Nile cataract; at the end of his section on Roman ruins he placed a view of Stonehenge contrasted with the theatre installed in rock in the garden of Hellbrunn Palace near Salzburg, and a prospect of Isola Bella on Lake Maggiore. In the section on Chinese monuments he included gardens with artificial rocks, and a suspension bridge audaciously stretched between two mountains. Such illustrations reveal Fischer's conception of the connection and interconnection between nature and art; that nature produces remarkable forms which sometimes resemble architecture and that man can, on the other hand, raise nature to the level of a work of art by making use of forms provided by nature.

Fischer's attitude towards antiquity was not that of a modern archaeologist, whose aim is to strip ancient monuments of all later accretions in order to produce a pure reconstruction, but of an architect with a lively interest in ancient forms. He saw himself as part of a living stream of architectural development and as one who was completing ideas which began in antiquity. This gave him not only the courage but also the justification to look at antiquity with his own eyes.

Although he did not carry out his plan to survey medieval architecture, he had for his time an unusually great interest in, and sympathetic understanding of, Gothic buildings – as, for example, his altar in the Franciscan Church in Salzburg [74] demonstrates. Here, too, he shows how far his attitude towards the architecture of the past was from being simply one of purism or of preservationism; because of this, he was able to create a harmonious union between medieval and Baroque works of art and architecture.

·3·
The Essence of Fischer's Architecture

Each of Fisher's works is composed of several different elements. He quite consciously brought contrasting features together and harmonized the heterogeneous parts into a unified whole. In each of his undertakings, he first considered the solutions that had already been found for the problem confronting him and formed his own work out of this material. In a highly idealistic synthesis of the achievements of past and present he tried to find a new, even unique solution for each task, the best of all possible solutions. In this respect, his ideas parallel the philosophy of Gottfried Wilhelm Leibniz, who regarded the world as the best of all possible worlds (though not of course in the sense later given to these words by Voltaire's Pangloss). Fischer's buildings are like Leibniz's ideas built in stone.

At first sight, this close link between architecture and philosophy may seem unusual. But Fischer was an artist of wide culture and universal interests, and Leibniz had many connections in Vienna. This universally learned man exerted an influence on three of Fischer's works while they were still in the planning stage: the Karlskirche, the academy of science, and the imperial library. Leibniz published no comprehensive philosophical treatise in his lifetime, but gave expression to his ideas in occasional essays. A key to his philosophical system can be found in his extensive correspondence with other philosophers and scientists. He attempted to reunite the Protestant and Catholic Churches and actively promoted the foundation of academies of science in Berlin, Vienna, St Petersburg and other European capitals. He was politically opposed to Louis XIV of France and was, from 1676 onwards, employed at the court of Hanover as political adviser and librarian and as historian of the Guelphs. Charles VI appointed Leibniz a *Reichshofrat* (a counsellor in one of the imperial courts of justice) in 1712 and from then until 1714 he stayed in Vienna, where he began writing his (posthumously published) philosophical system, *Monadology*. He gave to Prince Eugene of Savoy a concise summary of this work, written in his own hand and entitled *Principes de la Nature et de la Grâce fondés en Raison* (now in the Österreichische Nationalbibliothek, Vienna, Cod. 10. 588). After the death of Queen Anne and the accession of the Elector of Hanover to the English throne, however, he returned to Hanover, though he would have liked to have gone to London. He continued to correspond with Charles VI, Prince Eugene, Heraeus, and others at the Viennese court until he died in 1716.

It is not known when Fischer became acquainted with Leibniz's ideas. It is possible, but not very probable, that he was already familiar with them during the early 1690s, when he was producing his first great works. There is no doubt whatever, on the other hand, that his first project for Schönbrunn reveals close parallels with Leibniz's thought. But Fischer apparently reached quite independently a conception of architecture related to Leibniz's philosophy. It developed under the influence of the syntheticism of the Late Roman Baroque, the rise of modern archaeology, and the attempts made by French classical architects to harmonize contrasting elements. But it was determined most strongly by his own deeply idealistic attitude which compelled him to strive after absolute perfection in all his works. The direct influence of Leibniz's ideas on Fischer's works can be assumed from the first decade of the eighteenth century. But only in the case of the imperial architecture of Fischer's late period can this influence be proved by documentary evidence.

Fischer's theocentric conception of the world is reflected most clearly in his history of architecture: from the divinely inspired beginnings of architecture, in the orders of columns of Solomon's Temple, and by way of the Greek and Roman buildings, to his own work which he considered as the end of the development in 'orders'. Fischer's view of the world was ultimately based on the same concept of God as that which underlay Leibniz's philosophy: God was the greatest of all architects, who had created the world as a perfect building, as the best of all possible worlds. Both Leibniz and Fischer could be characterized as having a deep and optimistic trust in the order of the universe – which the philosopher expressed in his *Théodicée* of 1710. According to his hypothesis of harmony all finite substances are so fashioned, thanks to their common origin, that their movements correspond exactly with one another (*l'harmonie préétablie des substances*). These simple – bodily and spiritual –

substances, which could not be inwardly influenced or changed in any way by others, he called 'monads'; each body was an aggregate of many monads. He believed that these monads were emanations from God, the supreme and central monad; he reigned in his realm as a monarch over the other monads, which served him freely and happily in perfect order. In their belief in universal harmony, Leibniz and Fischer were among the last representatives of the old theocentric view of the universe in which God and the world, faith and knowledge, were still united. It is hardly surprising that Leibniz was unable to agree with Hobbes, Locke, and Newton (as his extensive correspondence with Samuel Clarke shows) and that Pierre Bayle attacked him in the *Dictionnaire historique et critique*. But it is easy to see why his ideas fell on fertile soil and were able to flourish in the imperial court at Vienna, where this great effort of human reason to re-unite the already diverging spheres was greatly esteemed. The universal order defended by Leibniz formed the spiritual basis for the position of the Emperor, the first representative of God's majesty on earth, who stood at the summit of a pyramid of princes and noblemen. Both Leibniz and Fischer served this hierarchy in their own ways, Leibniz as a politician, scientist and philosopher, Fischer as an architect. Both honoured and glorified the majesty of God and the majesty of the Emperor, which was firmly rooted in the divine order of the universe.

Fischer's basic architectural principle, which can be seen in each of his buildings with several different aspects, consisted in aggregating structural elements, without mutual fragmentation, in the interest of a higher unity formed by independent parts. This principle has much in common with Leibniz's doctrine of monads. Fischer's buildings, constructed from self-contained, individual elements so combined that they formed a harmonious whole, clearly make a constantly changing impression on the person who looks at them from different points of view. Leibniz similarly took the city, which also appears differently from various viewpoints, as his example for the universe. Although the infinite number of monads means, he taught, that there may seem to be infinite aggregations of different universes, there is nonetheless really only one universe, seen from the various viewpoints of the infinite number of individual monads. As a result there is the greatest possible diversity, but at the same time the greatest possible order in the universe, in other words, the greatest possible perfection (see Leibniz's *Monadology*, § 57, 58).

Just as Leibniz believed that God was the greatest architect who had created the best of all possible worlds, so Fischer endeavoured, in all his architectural creations, to find the perfect solution for each task from among the already existing possibilities. Essential for him was the conception of the whole, the harmonizing of the parts, which in themselves need not or could not be perfect. Leibniz too believed that a part of a beautiful whole need not be beautiful itself. In opposition to the encyclopaedist Bayle, who, following the French theory of art, insisted that it was more moral to prefer a comfortable to a splendid style of architecture, Leibniz replied that there were cases in which it was right to give preference to the beauty of the configuration of a palace rather than to its comfort (see his *Théodicée*, II, § 213-15). In his idealistic conceptions Fischer had often disregarded the occupants' demand for comfort and defied the reality of the climate. He only took into consideration the demands made by court ceremonial and the iconographical programme which would glorify the patron. This gave him the right to sacrifice comfort and practical considerations to the demands of an ideal ground-plan and the harmony of the whole building.

The idea of harmony was the underlying principle not only of Leibniz's metaphysics, but also of Fischer's architecture. Just as Leibniz attempted to reconcile opposites and to find a compromise between traditional philosophy and that of his own period – in which the ideas of the Renaissance were essential to his thought – Fischer tried to synthesize the contemporary styles of architecture and the classical tradition, regarding himself as the last representative product of the Renaissance. His synthesis was not a rigid system with unchanging parts; its elements changed according to the task in an attempt to find the best possible solution.

Like Leibniz, Fischer was a European in the true sense of the word, constantly in dialogue with the other great personalities of his time. His sources were found not only in the architecture of his masters of the preceding generations – the High and Late Roman Baroque – and of his contemporaries, but in the whole development of Renaissance and post-Renaissance architecture. In his constant recourse to antiquity, in his architectural play with regular geometrical forms, in the classical harmony of his buildings and in the universality of his interests, he was closer to the architects of the Italian Renaissance than any other Baroque architect. Though familiar with the French and English architecture of his own period and clearly influenced by it both in theory and in practice, he was not simply a 'modern' architect like his contemporaries. In Fischer's works the styles of the past – of antiquity, of sixteenth-century Italian and of mid-seventeenth-century French architecture – played a far greater part. His works were 'historical' architecture. None of his buildings exactly resembles another: each one is unique of its kind and inimitable.

Fischer's architecture cannot be seen in terms of a progressive development of his artistic personality. His first works in Austria are already mature. It is only possible to distinguish two periods in his career – before and after his visit to north Germany and England. Within these two periods we can observe a development only if we compare buildings of the same function: for his architecture was above all functional. The form of every building – the models that he chose for it and the way in which he transformed them – was determined by the function of the building and by the personality and social position of the patron. His collection of drawings and designs for 'recreational' architecture shows this clearly enough. But the individual forms have more than aesthetic value – they contain a deeper meaning as well. Fischer was endowed with an astonishing gift for expressing iconographical conceptions in an architectural form. In his church buildings these conceptions were used to glorify God or the saint to whom the church was dedicated. In his palaces their purpose was an apotheosis of the owner. In this way, even his secular buildings were raised almost to the status of 'sacred' architecture.

Fischer's idea of combining architecture and the figurative arts to form a *Gesamtkunstwerk* based on a unified intellectual conception was also in accordance with Leibniz's idea of harmony. The *Gesamtkunstwerk* of the Austrian Baroque, inaugurated in Fischer's works, was the last of its kind in Europe, the last in which a monumental architecture was the basis and the figurative arts were subordinated to it. (In French and south German Rococo it was confined to the interior of the building and the figurative arts were already beginning to destroy the architectonic structure. Classicism and Romanticism were no longer capable of producing a monumental *Gesamtkunstwerk*.) In Fischer's view, this *Gesamtkunstwerk* was not a self-contained whole, but something that had to be seen in the total context of townscape or landscape. All his buildings were designed with reference to their natural and artistic environment. They were not intended to be subordinate to their environment but to fit closely into it, giving it a new appearance and a new meaning. Fischer wanted his churches and his palaces to intensify and perfect nature, an aim which was ultimately religious and born of his faith in God's universal order.

Although he was so skilled at synthesizing different structural elements and so much enjoyed doing this that he produced buildings of very many different types, Fischer still managed to attain an extremely personal style. This individual style can best be characterized by certain leitmotifs which he varied again and again and which he used for different purposes. The most important are the domed oval, the main axis of which is the longitudinal; the

Raumtor mit Flügeln (or Liechtenstein belvedere motif); the paired triumphal columns with spiral reliefs; the 'diadem arch'; and the elegantly curved portal connected with the richly decorated window above. His architecture is eminently sculptural and full of dynamic contrasts between convex and concave forms. In this, he showed himself to be firmly rooted in the tradition of Bernini, as is revealed in a great number of his architectural inventions, especially in his altars, monuments and fountains, as well as in his style of drawing. As one who was born at a late period in history and trained in the Late Roman Baroque, he was bound to synthesize; the way in which he did this and the elements he chose for his synthesis demonstrate that he was a pupil of Bernini. It is true that he also took architectural details from Borromini and Guarini, but he studiously avoided their tendency to merge and fragment space. The basis of his architectural conception was the spatial element of simple ground-plan, which was not penetrated by other spaces so that its basic shape remained intact. The spatial elements were arranged so that the inner structure of a building could be clearly seen from outside – at least as far as free-standing buildings were concerned. In his churches as well as in his palaces he tried to reconcile the longitudinal and the central plan. Even his smaller buildings have a monumental effect because of the noble simplicity of their plans and the consistent use of the order. Sharply projecting cornices accentuate the lines of the ground-plan in all his works and tie together the spatial volumes. Not to detract from the monumental effect of his architecture, Fischer made sparse use of ornament; but dynamic sculpture forms an integral part of his architecture. He restricted illusionistic painting to ceilings.

What radically differentiates Fischer's architecture from that of his Roman High and Late Baroque masters is the symbolic meaning inherent in almost all of the forms he used. This fusion of form and content, of architecture, painting and sculpture, of different styles, of nature and art, demands that the spectator should both comprehend the individual elements and at the same time visualize them as a whole, in a subjective way. This subjectivity in a work of art, which implies a greater spiritual freedom, is a characteristic of art north of the Alps. The Italian Baroque work of art has a much more objective beauty; the French, English or north German work of art is much more rational. By remaining quite open to the influences of the past and the present, however, and attempting to bring them together to create something quite new, Fischer showed himself to be an Austrian in the best sense of the word and a true European besides.

This highly idealistic view of architecture, compelling Fischer to look among the various possibilities presented by the past and the present for the absolutely perfect solution to each of his architectural tasks, could only be developed and put into practice at this particular time and in this particular place and social situation – a situation based on political power and economic prosperity. The appearance of an architect with such wide-ranging interests coincided with a unique period in the history of Austria, when the danger from the Turks, which had threatened her for two centuries, had at last been removed and when, in confronting France, she had become a great power. At this period, when the idea of Empire was revived and cherished by the Habsburgs, the city of Vienna (where the Emperor resided) became a European centre of art and architecture again. This was mostly due to Fischer's achievements. Fischer worked exclusively for imperial and noble patrons and his architecture reflected the power of three successive emperors and a group of noblemen who vied with the imperial court in the building of impressive houses and monuments. This unique combination of political power, economic prosperity and congenial patrons made it possible, perhaps for the last time, for the idea of a *Gesamtkunstwerk* to be fulfilled in architecture. Austrian Baroque was born and, as it grew, gradually embraced the entire Habsburg Empire, even spreading into south Germany, where it had a deep influence on art and architecture. Its creator and prime mover was Fischer. Later Baroque architecture in Austria preserved the characteristics of his art – the notion of the *Gesamtkunstwerk*, the predilection for harmony, the antipathy to the fragmentation of space, and the close connection between art and nature. The monumental gravity of Fischer's architecture continued to have an effect for decades after his death, while the Rococo made little impact in Austria.

Despite all this Fischer had no immediate successors and founded no school. His architecture could not be taught, repeated or copied. In the strictest sense of the word his buildings were functional, determined by their purpose; his was, therefore, an architecture which was bound to live and die with the duties it fulfilled and with the political, social and economic situation which had produced it. In his own period Fischer occupied a lonely summit in Austria and perhaps even in Europe. The sculptors and painters who collaborated with him did not even remotely approach his artistic level. In Johann Michael Rottmayr, it is true, he found a painter who was very much in sympathy with his aims and who attempted to achieve a synthesis between the painting of the High and Late Roman Baroque and Flemish painting, especially that of Rubens. Rottmayr was responsible for the illusionistic frescoes decorating Fischer's main works [4, 23, 96] and was one of the founders of the Austrian school of Baroque painting. It is also true that sculptors of real ability worked on Fischer's buildings – Giovanni Giuliani [1, 46], Matthias Braun [84], Ferdinand Maximilian Brokoff [95, 97] and others. But none of these painters or sculptors ever attained the same universality or displayed the same intellectual wealth as Fischer did in his artistic conceptions.

Only those of Fischer's works which his contemporaries recognized as types had any direct influence on the architecture of the period. Johann Lucas von Hildebrandt took Fischer's garden palaces of the 1690s as a model for some of his early works. They also had an influence on architects in Bohemia, Moravia and south Germany. Hildebrandt and other Viennese architects were also influenced by the façades of Fischer's town palaces of the same period. The façade of the University Church in Salzburg, with its convex central section between the two towers, impressed the architects of a whole series of churches in south Germany and Switzerland. Schönbrunn, too, exerted an influence on several palaces in Germany. The greatest and most lasting effect, however, was made by Fischer's 'Palladian' palace façades, which, more than any of his other works, could be regarded as constituting a distinctive architectural type. This type of façade subsequently became widespread throughout the Habsburg Empire. Their portals, supported by atlantes, were also frequently imitated. Fischer's great church buildings and his imperial architecture, on the other hand, apparently had no successors at all.

It is interesting to note that Fischer's son, who grew up in his father's studio and completed many of his buildings, cannot in any sense be regarded as his immediate successor and disciple. While he was in Paris, he was so impressed by early eighteenth-century French architecture that it had a deep and lifelong influence on his work.

Johann Bernhard Fischer von Erlach was the founder of Austrian Baroque architecture, but it was left to other and less universal architects to give this period in Austria its distinctive character. It is to these men to whom we owe the familiar image of Austrian towns and the Austrian countryside. Some of Fischer's contemporaries and even more historians of art and architecture have preferred the more accommodating and pleasing and less pretentious architecture of Hildebrandt to that of Fischer. Hildebrandt certainly created a number of architectural types for different purposes, which were repeated later over a wide area, from south Germany to the Balkans. But only in a very few buildings did he create something really exceptional – for example, in the Belvedere in Vienna, the summer residence of Prince Eugene of Savoy (built 1714–22), and in his ideal design of 1718–19 for the monastery of Göttweig on a mountain by the Danube – only partly carried out.

Only one really outstanding work can be attributed to the third important architect of the Austrian Baroque, Jakob Prandtauer, and that is the Baroque rebuilding of the monastery of Melk on the Danube (begun in 1702). Donato Felice d'Allio's ideal design for the monastery of Klosterneuburg, the 'Austrian Escorial' (begun in 1730 and never completed), followed long after, both in time and in artistic quality. None of these buildings attained either the sublimity of Fischer's works, in which form and content were so consistently united, or the universality of his architectural aspirations.

In about 1730 the Emperor and the noblemen of Austria began to show very much less interest in building and architecture. The great age of Austria's rise to power was passing and the glory and splendour of the Habsburg Empire was fading. In the later years of his reign, Charles VI became involved in many different political and military conflicts in his attempts to ensure that his daughter, Maria Theresa, would succeed him. Wars with France and the Turks resulted in territorial losses and, even more important, loss of prestige. Maria Theresa had to fight for almost twenty years with Prussia for the survival of her Empire. The Habsburg Empire was gradually changing from an absolute state into a modern one during the reign of Charles VI and this transformation became more rapid and more complete in the time of Maria Theresa. It was during this period that Vienna lost its leading position as a great centre of architecture and that the important buildings came more and more to be erected in the provinces, especially by the Church and the local governments of the Habsburg territories. These buildings were certainly designed with some of Fischer's architectural principles and forms in mind, but they lacked the intellectual greatness of his conception and the historical and European aspect of his work.

It has often been said that architecture, more than any other art form, is determined by society. Fischer's work is a particularly striking example of the truth of this saying. The philosophy and outlook on the world of the ruling hierarchy of the Habsburg Empire, the last exponents of a whole order of society, are vividly reflected in Fischer's buildings. Nonetheless, his architecture was not simply and solely conditioned by society. In its claim to absolute perfection, it points beyond the demands made by society to something higher – to a theocentric view of the world and a universal order in which the Emperor and his hierarchy of princes and noblemen were rooted.

Appendix: Fischer as a Draughtsman

We possess a relatively large number of drawings connected with Fischer's works, but only a few of these are in fact his own sketches or designs. Most of them are preparatory designs for engravings and were certainly not all executed by him. There are also many drawings from his studio among the designs for his buildings – for example, a group of designs for his buildings in Salzburg, which are now kept either in the Landesarchiv or in the Museum Carolino Augusteum in Salzburg [e.g. 34]. The younger Fischer worked in his father's studio, but it is not yet possible to identify which drawings were executed by the father and which by the son.

The largest group of drawings, at least partly in Fischer's own hand, is made up of the preliminary designs for the plates in his history of architecture, into which were incorporated some already existing sheets for the series of engravings of his Salzburg buildings, as well as the 'Prospect of Schönbrunn Palace' which Fischer had published in 1701. This group of drawings is at present kept in three collections. Seventy-nine sheets are owned by the University Library of Zagreb (at present on loan to the Yugoslav Academy of Art and Science), four are in the library of the Oberösterreichisches Landesmuseum in Linz, and three are in the Museum Carolino Augusteum in Salzburg. Some of these drawings were not reproduced when the book was published, and some of Fischer's works are known only from drawings in the Zagreb collection [31, 56, 75]. Fischer's style of drawing was obviously very much influenced by the school of Bernini, as is clearly revealed in the sculptural details. The signature on some of the engravings reveals that Joseph Emanuel made a number of drawings of his father's buildings. Several different artists seem to have been responsible for the staffage figures, and the preliminary drawings for the engravings signed by the elder Fischer himself are not wholly or necessarily by his hand.

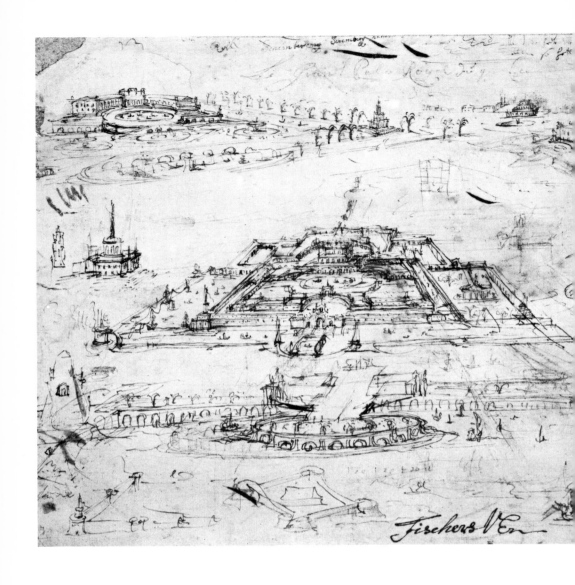

110. Projects and reconstructions (detail of drawing)

Much more of Fischer's personal way of working is revealed, however, in the *Codex Montenuovo*, a collection of drawings and designs for garden houses and palaces, in other words, of *architectura recreationis*, which he made himself and mounted on sheets of blue paper (Graphische Sammlung Albertina, Vienna [54, 59, 60, 67, 70, 110]). The volume contains Fischer's own designs as well as drawings of foreign buildings, some in his own hand and others made by different artists, and even etchings of garden palaces. Several designs for park gates, which are mounted on the same blue paper (Albertina, Vienna [3]), lead one to suppose that Fischer possessed other volumes for different architectural tasks – for park gates, vases, town palaces, church buildings, altars, sepulchral monuments, *Scheinarchitektur*, and perhaps even for fortified buildings and bridges. Corrections and variations are often marked by Fischer on his own designs and on those by other hands in the *Codex Montenuovo*. The drawings collected there extend over a period of more than twenty years. It was a 'working collection' of which Fischer made use over the years. His style of drawing differs according to the purpose of the sheet. There are, for example, preliminary drawings for engravings, especially the series of designs for small garden pavilions in Salzburg [59, 60], very carefully executed designs for other buildings [70], and also preparatory sketches. It is, of course, these hasty first sketches which best reveal Fischer's special characteristics. The most interesting sheet of drawings contains ideas for his history of architecture and for his own garden palaces [110]. Various designs (reconstructions and original works), more or less clearly recognizable, are placed beside and above each other. In the centre of the sheet there are the first ideas for his reconstruction of Nero's Domus Aurea. Below this are his sketches for the reconstruction of Domitian's *Naumachia*, to which the Temple of Nineveh is added. At the top, on the left, is a reduced version of the garden palace Fischer designed for Frederick I of Prussia, with a second *Naumachia* in front of it and a step pyramid on the right. Fischer used very bold strokes and had an exceptional gift for seizing hold of the characteristic shape and dynamism of a building, even in his most hastily executed sketches, and of anticipating with the most modest means the impression that would be made by the completed building.

Fischer's drawings on a larger scale, executed as designs for monuments, altars and fountains (Albertina, Vienna, and the archives of the Franciscan monastery in Salzburg), are works of art in their own right, less architectural designs than artistic visions. In these designs for structures richly decorated with sculpture Fischer is especially close to Bernini's style of drawing. The most perfect is his design for the high altar at Mariazell (formerly in the

Heymann Collection in Vienna, now in a German private collection [71]), in which every line seems to vibrate with his impression of the celestial vision.

But even in purely architectural designs, insofar as these were in his own hand, his style is never sober and dispassionate: on the contrary he is always bent on dynamic accentuation and contrast [3, 31]. A typical feature of these designs is his frequent use of delicate statues on the attic, their flamelike curves enlivening the straight line of the roof. The staffage that gives life to so many of his designs forms a gay and amusing chapter on its own – little caricatures and *genre* figures in the tradition of Stefano della Bella and Jacques Callot, but thoroughly Viennese in silhouette [70].

His style of drawing is basically that of a sculptor-architect who had a predilection for illusionistic effects and who regarded architecture not as an isolated phenomenon, but as a *Gesamtkunstwerk*.

Bibliographical Notes

General Works

Systematic research into Baroque architecture in Austria was initiated by A. Ilg, but only the first volume of his work on the Fischer family, *Die Fischer von Erlach*, the one dealing with the elder Fischer, was published (Vienna, 1895). Even today, it is indispensable as a collection of material. The basis for any modern research into Fischer must be H. Sedlmayr's monograph, *Johann Bernhard Fischer von Erlach* (Vienna and Munich, 1956; revised edition now in preparation), a very comprehensive study of Fischer's personality and work written after many years of preparatory study, listing all the documentary evidence and literature on the subject. At the same time as Sedlmayr's monograph appeared, the present author published the catalogue of the commemorative exhibition (H. Aurenhammer, *Johann Bernhard Fischer von Erlach – Ausstellung*, Graz, Vienna and Salzburg, 1956–7, 2nd impression, 1957), which contained an analysis of all Fischer's works, including historical evidence and a full bibliography. G. Kunoth's *Die Historische Architektur Fischers von Erlach* (Düsseldorf, 1956) should be consulted for any information about Fischer's archaeological reconstructions and about those of his works illustrated in his history of architecture. Since the jubilee year, several books and articles on individual works and problems have appeared. These are listed and discussed in R. Wagner-Rieger's critical bibliography in the *Zeitschrift für Kunstgeschichte*, 1964, p. 246 ff., which also provides an excellent survey of the research that has been done into Austrian Baroque architecture generally.

1. Fischer and his Time

The history of Austria in the seventeenth and eighteenth centuries: F. M. Mayer, *Geschichte Österreichs mit besonderer Rücksicht auf das Kulturleben*, II, Vienna, 1909; H. Hantsch, *Die Geschichte Österreichs*, II, Vienna, 3rd edn, 1962; H. Pirchegger, *Geschichte und Kulturleben Österreichs*, II, Vienna, 5th edn, 1960; E. Zöllner, *Geschichte Österreichs*, Vienna, 3rd edn, 1966; O. Redlich, *Weltmacht des Barock. Österreich in der Zeit Kaiser Leopolds*

I, Vienna, 4th edn, 1961; O. Redlich, *Das Werden einer Großmacht, Öster-reich 1700–1740*, Vienna, 4th edn, 1962; T. Schüssel, *Das Werden Öster-reichs*, Vienna and Munich, 1964; H. L. Mikoletzky, *Österreich. Das große 18. Jahrhundert*, Vienna, 1967; E. Tomek, *Kirchengeschichte Österreichs*, II, Vienna, 1949; J. Wodka, *Kirche in Österreich*, Vienna, 1959; M. Braubach, *Prinz Eugen von Savoyen*, 5 volumes, Vienna, 1963–5.

Cultural life in Austria during the seventeenth and eighteenth cen-turies: O. Redlich, 'Über Kunst und Kultur des Barocks in Österreich', *Archiv für Österreichische Geschichte*, 115, 1943/II, p. 333 ff; H. von Srbik, *Wien und Versailles 1692–97*, Munich, 1944; T. Schüssel, *Kultur des Barock in Österreich*, Graz, 1960; A. Coreth, *Pietas Austriaca*, Vienna, 1959; A. Hoffmann, 'Österreichs Wirtschaft im Zeitalter des Absolu-tismus', *Festschrift für K. Eder*, Innsbruck, 1959; F. Tremel, *Wirtschafts- und Sozialgeschichte Österreichs*, Vienna, 1969; R. A. Kann, *A Study in Austrian Intellectual History from Late Baroque to Romanticism*, New York, 1960.

Art and architecture in seventeenth- and eighteenth-century Austria: K. Ginhart, ed., *Die bildende Kunst in Österreich*, IV and V, Baden bei Wien, 1939; H. Tietze, *Wien. Kultur, Kunst, Geschichte*, Vienna, 1931; O. Benesch, *Kleine Geschichte der Kunst in Österreich*, Vienna, 1950; N. Powell, *From Baroque to Rococo, an Introduction to Austrian and German Architecture from 1580 to 1790*, London, 1959; B. Grimschitz, R. Feucht-müller, W. Mrazek, *Barock in Österreich*, Vienna, Hanover, and Basle, 1960; E. Hempel, *Baroque Art and Architecture in Central Europe*, Pelican History of Art, Harmondsworth, 1965; R. Wagner-Rieger, 'Il Palla-dianismo in Austria', *Bollettino del Centro Internazionale di Studi di Architettura Andrea Palladio*, VII/2, 1965, p. 77 ff; R. Wagner-Rieger, 'Die Baukunst des 16. und 17. Jahrhunderts in Österreich. Ein For-schungsbericht', *Wiener Jahrbuch für Kunstgeschichte*, XX (XXIV), 1965, p. 175 ff; R. Wagner-Rieger, 'Das Verhältnis J. B. Fischers von Erlach zur österreichischen Architektur', *Alte und Moderne Kunst*, III, 1958, no. 4, p. 12 ff.

The city of Graz and Fischer's father: R. Meeraus, 'Die Werkstatt Johann Baptist Fischers', *Blätter für Heimatkunde von Steiermark*, 1927, no. 2; R. Kohlbach, *Die barocken Kirchen von Graz*, Graz, 1951; R. Kohlbach, *Steirische Bildhauer*, Graz, 1956; R. Kohlbach, *Steirische Baumeister*, Graz, 1961; K. Woisetschläger, ed., *Der Grazer Hofkünstler Pietro de Pomis*, Graz, 1973 (= Joannea, Publikationen des Steier-märkischen Landesmuseums Joanneum, II).

Queen Christina of Sweden, Roman archaeologists, and seventeenth-century art theory: L. Grottanelli, *La regina Cristina di Svezia in Roma*, Florence, 2nd edn, 1908; F. Boyer, 'Les antiques de Christine de Suède à Rome', *Revue archéologique*, 5:35, 1932, p. 254 ff; C. Callmer, *Drottning Kristinas samlingar av antik konst*, Stockholm, 1954 (= Svenska humanis-tiska förbundet, Skrifter 63); S. Stolpe, *Queen Christina of Sweden*, London, 1965; P. Bjurström, ed., *Christina Queen of Sweden*, Catalogue of the 11th Exhibition of the Council of Europe, Stockholm, 1966; P. Bonanni, *Museum Kircherianum*, Rome, 1709; N. Seng, *Die Selbstbiographie des P. Athanasius Kircher aus der Gesellschaft Jesu*, Fulda, 1901; J. J. Walsh, *Catholic Churchmen in Science*, Philadelphia, 1906; P. Friedländer, *Athana-*

sius Kircher und Leibniz. Ein Beitrag zur Geschichte der Polyhistorie im 17. Jahrhundert, first published 1937, reprinted in: P. Friedländer, *Studien zur antiken Literatur und Kunst*, Berlin, 1969; E. Panofsky, '*Idea*', *ein Beitrag zur Begriffsgeschichte der älteren Kunsttheorie*, Berlin, 1924, 2nd edn, 1960 (on Bellori); N. Pevsner, *Academies of Art*, Cambridge, 1940; D. Mahon, *Studies in Seicento Art and Theory*, London, 1947; H. H. Rhys, ed., *Seventeenth Century Science and the Arts*, Princeton, 1961; R. Wittkower, *Architectural Principles in the Age of Humanism*, London, 3rd edn, 1962.

Fischer, Bernini, and the Schors: H. Sedlmayr, 'Fischer von Erlach und Bernini', *Das Münster*, 1952, p. 265 ff; G. Aurenhammer, *Die Handzeichnung des 17. Jahrhunderts in Österreich*, Vienna, 1958, pp. 12 ff., 103 ff; N. Wibiral, 'Contributi alle ricerche sul Cortonismo in Roma', *Bollettino d'Arte*, 1960, p. 144 ff.

Fischer and French architecture: P. Moisy, 'Fischer von Erlach et les architectes français', *Art de France*, III, 1963, p. 154 ff.

Fischer as a sculptor, medallist, and designer for the arts: F. Dworschak, 'Der Medailleur Johann Bernhard Fischer von Erlach', *Jahrbuch der kunsthistorischen Sammlungen in Wien*, 1934, p. 234 ff; J. Schmidt, 'Johann Bernhard Fischer von Erlach als Bildhauer', *Belvedere*, XIII, 1938-9, p. 2 ff; M. Dreger, 'Zu Känischbauer und der Barockplastik in Österreich', *Kunst und Kunsthandwerk*, 1915, p. 529 ff; H. Tietze, 'Beiträge zur Geschichte der österreichischen Barockarchitektur', *Kunst und Kunsthandwerk*, 1918, p. 402 ff; B. Thomas, 'Zwei Vorzeichnungen zu kaiserlichen Garde-Stangenwaffen von Hans Stromaier 1577 und Johann Bernhard Fischer von Erlach 1705', *Jahrbuch der kunsthistorischen Sammlungen in Wien*, LXV, 1969, p. 61 ff; G. Schikola, *Wiener Plastik der Renaissance und des Barocks*, Vienna, 1970, p. 102 ff (= Geschichte der bildenden Kunst in Wien. Die Plastik in Wien. Geschichte der Stadt Wien N.R., vol. VII, 1); G. Schikola, 'Ludovico Burnacinis Entwürfe für die Wiener Pestsaüle', *Wiener Jahrbuch für Kunstgeschichte*, XXV, 1972, p. 247 ff.

Fischer's works in Graz and Eisgrub (Lednice): H. Egger, 'Erstlingswerke J. B. Fischers von Erlach in der Steiermark', *Zeitschrift des Historischen Vereins für Steiermark*, XXVI, 1931, p. 248 ff; E. Hempel, 'Jugendwerke Fischers von Erlach', *Kunstchronik*, X, 1957, p. 338 ff; F. Wilhelm, 'Bauherr und Architekt des Reitstallgebäudes in Eisgrub', *Wiener Jahrbuch für Kunstgeschichte*, 1930, p. 28 ff; V. Fleischer, *Fürst Carl Eusebius von Liechtenstein als Bauherr und Kunstsammler (1611-1684)*, Vienna and Leipzig, 1910; W. Götz, *Deutsche Marställe des Barock*, Munich, 1964, p. 17 ff; [E. Charvátová and B. Storm], *Lednice, Státní Zámek*, Prague, 1963.

Fischer's family and his activity as inspector of court buildings: *Quellen zur Geschichte der Stadt Wien*, 1/6, nos. 7038, 7203, 9564, 9578, 9694, 11263, 11291, 12492; W. Pillich, 'Kunstregesten aus den Hofparteienprotokollen des Obersthofmeisteramtes von 1637-1780', *Mitteilungen des Österreichischen Staatsarchivs XII*, 1959, nos. 165, 167, and *XIII*, 1960, nos. 189, 191, 192, 302; C. List, 'J. B. Fischer von Erlach und der Strudel bei Grein', *Monatsblatt des Alterthums-Vereines zu Wien*, 1896, p. 9 ff.

Salzburg: F. Martin, *Kunstgeschichte von Salzburg,* Vienna, 1925; F. Martin, *Salzburgs Fürsten in der Barockzeit,* Salzburg, 1949; F. Fuhrmann, *Kirchen in Salzburg,* Vienna, 1949; F. Fuhrmann, *Salzburg in alten Ansichten,* Salzburg, 1963; R. K. Donin, *Vincenzo Scamozzi und der Einfluß Venedigs auf die Salzburger Architektur,* Innsbruck and Vienna, 1948; see also R. Wagner-Rieger's Italian article on Palladian architecture in Austria, mentioned above.

Prague, Bohemia, and Moravia: B. Knox, *Bohemia and Moravia, An Architectural Companion,* London, 1962; H. G. Franz, *Die Bauten und Baumeister der Barockzeit in Böhmen,* Leipzig, 1962; H. G. Franz, *Die deutsche Barockbaukunst Mährens,* Munich, 1943; J. Morper, 'Der Prager Architekt Jean-Baptiste Mathey', *Münchner Jahrbuch für Kunstgeschichte,* 1927, p. 99 ff; V. Richter, 'Fischeriana', *Umění,* 1962, p. 507 ff; K. M. Swoboda, ed., *Barock in Böhmen,* Munich, 1964; O. Blažíček, *Barockkunst in Böhmen,* Prague, 1967; J. Neumann, *Das böhmische Barock,* Prague, 1970.

Fischer in Venice: A. Ress, 'Fischer von Erlach in Venedig', *Kunstchronik,* X, 1957, p. 357 ff; R. K. Donin, 'Wiener Bauten des J. B. Fischer von Erlach und sein Aufenthalt in Venedig', *Jahrbuch des Vereins für Geschichte der Stadt Wien,* XV/XVI, 1959-60, p. 157 ff; T. Temanza, *Zibaldone,* ed. N. Ivanoff (= Fondazione Cini, Fonti e Testi, 3), Venice, 1963, pp. 20, 22.

Fischer's journey to Berlin, Holland, and England: H. Hantsch, 'Ein Berliner Aufenthalt J. B. Fischers von Erlach', *Belvedere,* 1927, p. 159 ff; G. Kühn in *Zeitschrift für Kunstgeschichte,* 1933, p. 152 ff; J. Schmidt, 'Die Architekturbücher der Fischer von Erlach', *Wiener Jahrbuch für Kunstgeschichte,* 1934, p. 152 ff; W. Ensingbach, 'Ein neuer Brief Fischers von Erlach', *Forschung und Fortschritte,* 1963, p. 378.

Leibniz, Heraeus, and Adolph von Albrecht at the court of Charles VI: J. Bergmann, *Sitzungsberichte der kaiserlichen Akademie der Wissenschaften in Wien,* phil.-hist. Klasse, XIII, 1854, pp. 40 ff., 539 ff; XVI, 1855, pp. 3 ff., 132 ff; and XXVI, 1858, p. 187 ff; E. F. Roessler, ibid., XX, 1856, p. 279; O. Klopp, *Archiv für Österreichische Geschichte,* XL, 1869, p. 246 ff; A. Lhotsky, *Festschrift des Kunsthistorischen Museums in Wien,* Vienna, 1941-5, especially volume II/I, p. 387 ff; M. Braubach, *Prinz Eugen von Savoyen,* V, Vienna, 1965, p. 171 ff; E. P. Garrettson's thesis on Conrad Adolph von Albrecht (Chicago University) will be published in the *Mitteilungen der Österreichischen Galerie,* Vienna.

The younger Fischer: J. Schmidt, 'Fischer von Erlach der Jüngere', *Mitteilungen des Vereins für Geschichte der Stadt Wien,* XIII/XIV, 1933, p. 84 ff; T. Zacharias, *Joseph Emanuel Fischer von Erlach,* Vienna and Munich, 1960.

2. Fischer's Works

It is advisable to consult the general works mentioned above for each one of Fischer's works. Only monographs on individual works or groups of works by Fischer and studies which have been published since the books by Sedlmayr, Kunoth, and the author are listed below.

a) K. Bielohlawek, 'Die Baudaten von J. B. Fischers von Erlach Belvedere Liechtenstein', *Monatsblatt des Vereins für Geschichte der Stadt Wien*, 1929–33, p. 1 ff; N. Knopp, *Das Garten-Belvedere*, Munich and Berlin, 1966; K. Bielohlawek, 'Fischer von Erlach und das Bergschloß Frain', *Wiener Jahrbuch für Kunstgeschichte*, 1926, p. 150 ff; T. Kubátová and A. Bartušek, *Vranov nad Dyjí*, Prague, 2nd edn, 1957; T. Kubátová and A. Bartušek, *Zprávy památkové péce*, XVII, 1957, p. 193 ff; H. Haselberger-Blaha, 'Die Triumphtore Fischers von Erlach', *Wiener Jahrbuch für Kunstgeschichte*, XVII, 1956, p. 63 ff; O. Raschauer, *Schönbrunn*, Vienna, 1960; see also H. Sedlmayr's article in the *Jahrbuch für Landeskunde von Niederösterreich*, NF XXXV/2, 1964, p. 696 ff; for the fountain in Brno, see two articles by J. Leisching in *Mitteilungen des Mährischen Gewerbemuseums in Brünn*, 1897, and in the *Zeitschrift des deutschen Vereins für die Geschichte Mährens und Schlesiens*, 1913, respectively, as well as the articles by M. Stehlik and H. Rokyta in J. Cervinka, ed., *J. B. Fischer von Erlach*, Brno, 1960 (Edice Medailony, I), p. 22 ff.

b) *Österreichische Kunsttopographie*, IX, pp. 160 ff., 235 ff., 256 ff., 271 ff; XIII, pp. 134 ff., 226 ff; XXV, p. 130 ff; M. Dreger, 'Zu den Salzburger Kirchenbauten Fischers von Erlach', *Wiener Jahrbuch für Kunstgeschichte*, 1929, p. 309 ff; L. Pretzell, *Fischer von Erlach in Salzburg* (= Führer zu großen Baudenkmälern, Heft 69), Berlin, 1944; F. Hagen-Dempf, *Die Kollegienkirche in Salzburg*, Vienna, 1949; F. Fuhrmann, 'Unveröffentlichte Archivalien zu J. B. Fischers von Erlach Tätigkeit in Salzburg', *Jahresschrift des Salzburger Museums Carolino Augusteum*, 1955 (1956), p. 30 ff; F. Fuhrmann, 'Neue Funde in Salzburg und ihre Bedeutung für das Werk und die Kenntnis Fischers von Erlach', *Kunstchronik*, X, 1957, p. 353 ff; *Maria Kirchenthal* (= Christliche Kunststätten Österreichs, vol. XXXIII), Salzburg, 1962; H. Fillitz, 'Die Kollegienkirche in Salzburg. Ihr Verhältnis zur römischen Architektur des 17. Jahrhunderts', *Wiener Jahrbuch für Kunstgeschichte*, XXV, 1972, p. 259 ff.

c) D. Frey, 'J. B. Fischer von Erlach. Eine Studie über seine Stellung in der Entwicklung der Wiener Palastfassade', *Wiener Jahrbuch für Kunstgeschichte*, 1921–2, p. 117 ff; B. Grimschitz, *Wiener Barockpaläste*, Vienna, 1944; H. Keller, *Das Treppenhaus im deutschen Schloß- und Klosterbau des Barock*, Munich, 1929; J. Fleischer, 'Umbau und Innenausstattung des Palais Stratmann-Windischgraetz in Wien', *Kunstgeschichtliche Studien* (= Festschrift D. Frey), ed. H. Tintelnot, Breslau, 1943, p. 45 ff; V. Hofmann von Wellenhof, *Der Winterpalast des Prinzen Eugen von Savoyen*, Vienna, undated; F. Windisch-Graetz, 'Urkunden zur Geschichte des Palais Batthyány-Schönborn in Wien', *Wiener Jahrbuch für Kunstgeschichte*, XVII, 1956, p. 116 ff.

d) H. Sedlmayr, 'Zum Oeuvre Fischers von Erlach', *Belvedere*, 1932, Heft 9/10 and 11/12; A. Ilg, 'Das Schloß Neuwaldegg', *Monatsblatt des Altherthums-Vereines zu Wien*, 1889, p. 59 ff; I. Williams Gregg, 'Der Grundriß des ehemaligen Palais Althann in der Roßau', *Wiener Jahrbuch für Kunstgeschichte*, XVII, 1956, p. 109 ff; L. Hautecoeur, 'Boffrand et le Plan en X', *Archives de l'art français, Nouvelle période*, XXII (= Mélanges G. Brière), 1959, p. 166 ff; G. Passavant, *Studien über Domenico Egidio Rossi und seine baukünstlerische Tätigkeit innerhalb des süddeutschen und österreichischen Barock*, Karlsruhe, 1967, p. 147 ff., 187f; *Österreichische Kunsttopographie*, II, p. XIV ff; O. Raschauer, *Schönbrunn*, Vienna, 1960; F. Martin, 'Schloß Klesheim', *Wiener Jahrbuch für Kunstgeschichte*, IV (XVIII), 1926, p. 176 ff; H. Sedlmayr, 'Bemerkungen zu Schloß Klesheim', *Mitteilungen der Gesellschaft für Salzburger Landeskunde*, CIX, 1969, p. 253 ff; H. Sedlmayr, 'Entwürfe Fischers von Erlach für ein Lustschloß Friedrichs I von Preussen', *Jahrbuch der Preussischen Kunstsammlungen*, 1932, p. 57 ff.

e) P. O. Wonisch, 'Der Hochaltar J. B. Fischers von Erlach in Mariazell', *St Lambrechter Quellen und Abhandlungen*, I/l, Graz, 1928; P. O. Wonisch, *Beschreibung der Mariazeller Sehenswürdigkeiten*, Mariazell, 1950; H. Haselberger-Blaha, op. cit. (see above, *a*), p. 70 ff; J. Schmidt, 'Fischer von Erlach als Bildhauer', *Belvedere*, XII, 1938-9, p. 7 ff; P. B. Gritsch, O.F.M., 'Zur Geschichte des Hochaltars in der Franziskanerkirche zu Salzburg', *Mitteilungen der Gesellschaft für Salzburger Landeskunde*, 1923-4, p. 153 ff; L. Popelka, 'Trauergerüste, Bemerkungen zu einer ephemeren Architekturgattung', *Römische Historische Mitteilungen*, X, 1966-7, p. 184 ff; L. Popelka, 'Das Trauergerüst der Wiener Universität für Kaiser Joseph I', *Wiener Jahrbuch für Kunstgeschichte*, XXIII, 1970, p. 239 ff.

f) D. Frey, op. cit. (see above, *c*), p. 147 ff., and the books by Grimschitz and Keller, op. cit. (see above, *c*); E. Leithe-Jasper, 'Archivalien zur Baugeschichte des Palais der Böhmischen Hofkanzlei in Wien', *Österreichische Zeitschrift für Kunst und Denkmalpflege,* XXI, 1967, p. 54 ff; J. Fleischer, 'Das Gartenpalais Trautson', *Belvedere*, 1929, Heft 9/10, p. 291 ff; M. Koller, 'Untersuchungen am Palais Trautson in Wien: Zu ursprünglicher Baugestalt, Fassadenfärbelung und Innendekoration', *Österreichische Zeitschrift für Kunst und Denkmalpflege*, XXII, 1968, p. 206 ff; E. Weber-Zeithammer, 'Studien über das Verhältnis von Architektur und Plastik in der Barockzeit, Untersuchungen an Wiener Palais des 17. und 18. Jahrhunderts', *Wiener Jahrbuch für Kunstgeschichte*, XXI, 1968, p. 158 ff; A. Kubiček, *The Palaces of Prague*, Prague, 1946, p. 126 ff; D. Libal and A. Beisetzer, *Jan Bernard Fischer z Erlachu a Clam-Gallasův palác v Praze*, Prague, 1956.

g) M. Dreger, 'Zur Baugeschichte der Wiener Karlskirche', *Wiener Jahrbuch für Kunstgeschichte*, 1934, p. 101 ff; L. Popelka, 'Studien zur Wiener Karlskirche', *Alte und Neue Kunst*, IV, 1955, p. 75 ff; E. Boeck, 'Die Frontalperspektive der Karlskirche in der "Historischen Architektur" von Johann Bernhard Fischer von Erlach', *Alte und Neue Kunst*, IV, 1955, p. 65 ff; H. Sedlmayr, 'Die Schauseite der Karlskirche in Wien', *Kunstgeschichtliche Studien für Hans Kauffmann*, Berlin, 1956, p. 262 ff. (Hans Sedlmayr has also written about the same problem in his *Epochen und Werke*, Vienna, 1960, II, pp. 174 ff., 243 ff); T. Zacharias, *Joseph Emanuel Fischer von Erlach*, Vienna and Munich, 1960, pp. 97 ff., 69 ff; R. Wagner-Rieger, 'Die Pragmatische Sanktion und die Kunst', *Der Donauraum*, IX, 1964, p. 67 ff; H. Foramitti has taken measurements of the Karlskirche by photogrammetry and published the results in *Société Française de Photogrammetrie*, *Bulletin*, no. 19, p. 22, plate 1, and in the *Deutsche Bauzeitung*, C, October 1966, Heft 10, p. 878, fig. 16, but so far they have not been exploited by art history; F. D. Fergusson, 'St Charles'

Church, Vienna: The Iconography of its Architecture', *Journal of the Society of Architectural Historians*, XXIX, 1970, p. 318 ff; St. Mossakowski, 'Die Kurfürstenkapelle Fischers von Erlach im Breslauer Dom', *Wiener Jahrbuch für Kunstgeschichte*, XIX (XXIII), 1962, p. 64 ff; W. Götz, *Deutsche Marställe des Barock*, Munich, 1964, p. 25 f; *Österreichische Kunsttopographie*, XIV; H. Kühnel, *Die Hofburg zu Wien*, Graz and Cologne, 1964; H. Kühnel, *Die Hofburg* (=Wiener Geschichtsbücher, vol. 5), Vienna and Hamburg, 1971; W. Buchowiecki, *Der Barockbau der ehemaligen Hofbibliothek in Wien, ein Werk Johann Bernhard Fischers von Erlach*, Vienna, 1957; Salomon Kleiner, *Eigentliche Vorstellung der vortrefflichen und kostbaren Kaiserlichen Bibliotec*, facsimile edition, edited and with a commentary by W. Buchowiecki (=*Wiennerisches Welttheater, Das barocke Wien in Stichen von Salomon Kleiner*, vol. I), Graz, 1967.

h) Entwurff Einer Historischen Architectur, facsimile edition of the 1725 Leipzig edition with the text of the 1730 London edition, Ridgewood, New Jersey (The Gregg Press Inc.), 1964; J. Schmidt, 'Die Architekturbücher der Fischer von Erlach', *Wiener Jahrbuch für Kunstgeschichte*, 1934, p. 149 ff; G. Kunoth, *Die Historische Architektur Fischers von Erlach*, Düsseldorf, 1956; E. Iversen, 'Fischer von Erlach as Historian of Architecture', *The Burlington Magazine*, C, 1958, p. 323 ff.

3. The Essence of Fischer's Architecture

H. Aurenhammer, *Johann Bernhard Fischer von Erlach*, Vienna, 1957 (=Österreich-Reihe, vols. 35-7); F. Heer, 'Weltbaukunst', *Alte und Moderne Kunst*, II, 1957, no. 1, p. 5 ff; for an introduction to the philosophy of Leibniz, see H. W. Carr, *Leibniz*, New York, 1929 (reprinted 1960); see also R. W. Meyer, *G. W. Leibnitz and the Seventeenth Century Revolution*, Cambridge, 1952; J. O. Fleckenstein, *G. W. Leibniz, Barock und Universalismus*, Thun and Munich, 1958; Y. Belaval, *Leibniz*, Paris, 1962; for the essence of Fischer's architecture, see H. Sedlmayr, 'Die europäische Bedeutung Johann Bernhard Fischers von Erlach', *Kunstchronik*, X, 1957, p. 334 ff; H. Sedlmayr, *Österreichische Barockarchitektur, 1690–1740*, Vienna, 1930; D. Frey, 'Zur Wesensbestimmung des österreichischen Barock', *Festschrift für H. Jantzen*, Berlin, 1951, p. 179 ff; W. Hager, 'Zum Verhältnis Fischer-Guarini', *Kunstchronik*, X, 1957, p. 206 ff. (the present author does not agree with Hager's view in most respects); R. Wagner-Rieger, 'Borromini und Österreich', *Atti del Convegno Borrominiano*, Rome, 1967; B. Grimschitz, *Johann Lucas von Hildebrandt*, Vienna and Munich, 1959; B. Grimschitz, 'Hildebrandt und Fischer', *Kunstchronik*, X, 1957, p. 341 ff; H. Aurenhammer, 'Begegnung der Rivalen', *Alte und Moderne Kunst*, II, 1957, no. 7/8, p. 7 ff; E. Hubala, 'Schleißheim und Schönbrunn', *Kunstchronik*, X, 1957, p. 349 ff; T. Zacharias, *Joseph Emanuel Fischer von Erlach*, Vienna and Munich, 1960.

Appendix: Fischer as a Draughtsman

M. Dreger, 'Zeichnungen des älteren Fischer von Erlach', *Kunstgeschichtliches Jahrbuch der k. k. Zentralkommission*, III, 1908, p. 139 ff; H. Folnesics, 'Neu aufgefundene Architekturzeichnungen und Risse zu

Salzburger Bauten', *Kunstgeschichtliches Jahrbuch der k. k. Zentralkommission*, 1915, Beiblatt, p. 42 ff; H. Tietze, 'Beiträge zur Geschichte der österreichischen Barockarchitektur', *Kunst und Kunsthandwerk*, XXI, 1918, p. 402 ff; J. Leisching, 'Handzeichnungen des älteren Fischer von Erlach', *Jahrbuch für Kunstwissenschaft*, XVI, 1923, p. 263 ff; H. Sedlmayr, 'Zum Oeuvre J. B. Fischers von Erlach' (see above, *d*); A. Schneider, 'J. B. Fischers von Erlach Handzeichnungen für den "Entwurff Einer Historischen Architectur"', *Zeitschrift für Kunstgeschichte*, I, 1932, p. 249 ff.

Chronological List of Fischer's Works

This list contains all the works for which documentary evidence exists, even those works which no longer exist themselves. It also includes those works which are attributed to him when these attributions are universally acknowledged. In the case of each work, the engravings which were made from drawings by Fischer or his son and which refer to the work in question are indicated, as well as the collections in which drawings by Fischer himself or from his studio are to be found.

Abbreviations

Albertina AZ: Vienna, Graphische Sammlung Albertina, Architektur-
    zeichnungen (architectural drawings).
Albertina CM: Vienna, Graphische Sammlung Albertina, Codex Monte-
    nuovo, Inv. No. 26392 (numbering of pages according to Sedlmayr).
D (Ds): drawing (drawings).
E (Es): engraving (engravings).
HA: Johann Bernhard Fischer von Erlach's 'History of Architecture'
    (*Entwurff Einer Historischen Architectur*, Vienna, 1721). The Roman
    numbers indicate the books, the Arabic numerals the plates.
P: Joseph Emanuel Fischer's 'Views of Some Viennese Buildings'
    (*Prospekte und Abriße einiger Gebäude von Wien*, Vienna, 1715). The
    numbers of the plates are in arabic numerals.
Salzburg LA: Salzburg, Landesarchiv, Bauamtsmappen IV – Alte
    Bauamtsakten K IV ad Nr 5 – Karten und Risse K 55.
Salzburg MCA: Salzburg, Museum Carolino Augusteum.
Zagreb: Zagreb University Library (numbering of the drawings accord-
    ing to Schneider and Sedlmayr).

1679 Bronze medal of King Charles II of Spain (attribution). Vienna,
    Kunsthistorisches Museum, Bundessammlung von Medaillen, Münzen,
    und Geldzeichen.

1682 Bronze medal of King Charles II of Spain and his first consort, Maria Ludovica of Bourbon. Vienna, Kunsthistorisches Museum, Bundessammlung von Medaillen, Münzen und Geldzeichen.

1687-9 Collaboration in the column dedicated to the Holy Trinity (Dreifaltigkeitssäule or Pestsäule), commemorating Vienna's deliverance from the plague and built on the Graben in Vienna; plans for alterations to the project after which the pedestal was carried out; model for the statue of Leopold I, not accepted and not preserved; six marble reliefs with biblical scenes on the pedestal, completed by Johann Ignaz Bendl.

1687 Design for the stucco decoration of the mausoleum of Emperor Ferdinand II in Graz.

Between 1687 and 1689 Bronze medal of the imperial court architect Lodovico Ottavio Burnacini and ivory portrait medallion appertaining to it (attribution). Vienna, Kunsthistorisches Museum, Bundessammlung von Medaillen, Münzen und Geldzeichen; medallion lost.

1687/8-90 Garden of the Prince of Liechtenstein in the Roßau in Vienna: belvedere (not preserved). E: HA V/12; designs for the garden (attribution; not preserved) and for park gates. E: HA V/13; Ds: Albertina AZ, Zagreb, no. 8.

1687-90 Designs for vases. Some were carried out later: Schloss Greillenstein, Lower Austria; park of the Schwarzenberg Palace in Vienna; church of the former Augustine convent of Dürnstein in Lower Austria. Es: HA V/11, 12, 13; Ds: Zagreb, nos. 8, 9.

Between 1687 and 1692 Design for the high altar of the pilgrimage church of Straßengel near Graz, Styria (not carried out). D: Albertina AZ.

1688 Designs for the stables of the Prince of Liechtenstein's palace, Schloss Eisgrub in Moravia (now Lednice in Czechoslovakia).

1688 Design for a park, snuff box and small-scale sculpture for Prince Maximilian Jakob Moriz von Liechtenstein (not preserved).

c. **1688** Model (in lead) for a medal of an unknown man, probably a self-portrait (attribution). Art collection of the Benediktinerstift Göttweig, Lower Austria.

1688-95 Great or 'Ancestral' Hall of Schloss Frain in Moravia (now Vranov nad Dyjí, Czechoslovakia).

1689/90 Reshaping of the park of Schloss Mirabell in Salzburg: designs for the park, for the entrance formed by statues of gladiators, and for vases (attribution).

c. **1690** Plan for a Grosses Landgebäude or mountain castle (not carried out). E: HA V/11; Ds: Albertina CM, fol. 21 verso, 22; Albertina AZ, Zagreb, nos. 65, 66.

1690 Two triumphal arches for Joseph I's entry into Vienna. Ds: Albertina AZ, Zagreb, nos. 75, 77.

1690 Preliminary drawings for the illustrations of *Arcus Triumphalis Leopoldo Magno Eleonorae Augustae Josepho Glorioso* ..., Vienna; (views of the triumphal arches and their emblems; preserved only in engravings).

c. **1690** First project for Schönbrunn Palace, outside Vienna (not carried out). E: HA IV/2; Ds: CM, fol. 16 verso, Zagreb, no. 74.

1690-96 Fountain in the Krautmarkt (nám. 25. února) in Brno, Czechoslovakia. Ds: Albertina AZ, Zagreb, no. 56.

1692/3 Palais Stratmann, Vienna (attribution). E: P 9.

1692-7 Hunting lodge Neuwaldegg, near Vienna (now Vienna XVII) (attribution). E: P 27.

1690-93 Summer riding school of the Archbishop's stables, Salzburg (attribution).

1692-1704 High altar of the pilgrimage church of Mariazell in Styria. E: C. Engelbrecht and J. A. Pfeffel after Johann Bernhard Fischer von Erlach; D: private collection in Germany, formerly in the Heymann Collection, Vienna.

1693/4 Façade, portal and horse pond of the Archbishop's stables, Salzburg.

c. **1693** Hunting lodge Engelhartstetten (Niederweiden) in the Marchfeld, Lower Austria. E: C. Engelbrecht and J. A. Pfeffel after Johann Bernhard Fischer von Erlach; D: anonymous drawing, Karlsruhe, Staatliche Kunsthalle, Collection of Plans.

c. **1693** Gartenpalais Althann in the Roßau, Vienna (not preserved; attribution). E: P 26; D: anonymous drawing, formerly in the possession of Domenico Egidio Rossi, now Karlsruhe, Staatliche Kunsthalle, Collection of Plans.

1694-1702 Dreifaltigkeitskirche (Church of the Holy Trinity) and priests' house (college building), Salzburg. Ds: Zagreb, no. 52, Salzburg MCA and LA.

1694-7 Spiral staircase in the north tower of the Cathedral, Salzburg.

1694 Garden pavilion ('Hoyoshaus') in the pheasantry of Klesheim Park near Salzburg. D: Albertina CM, fol. 10.

c. **1694** Seven other designs for garden pavilions. Ds: Albertina CM, fol. 4-9, 11; at one time there were also drawings of this kind in the Harrach collection, Vienna.

c. **1694** Plan for a star-shaped, fortified Landgebäude or country house (not carried out). E: HA IV/20; Ds: Albertina CM, fol. 21, 21a verso, Zagreb, nos. 67, 68.

c. **1694** Plan for a star-shaped chapel near Salzburg (not carried out; attribution). E: C. de la Haye, after a drawing in Albertina AZ.

Before 1695-1704 Hospital and Church of St John the Baptist (Johannes-Spital) in Salzburg. Ds: Salzburg LA and MCA.

1695 Design for the high altar of the mausoleum of Emperor Ferdinand II in Graz (attribution).

c. **1695** Gartenpalais Eckardt in the Josefstadt, Vienna (not preserved; attribution). Es: issued by the publishing office of Jeremias Wolff of Augsburg, perhaps engraved after drawings by Johann Bernhard Fischer von Erlach.

c. **1695** Plan for a Lustgebäude or pleasure house (not carried out). E: HA V/10; Ds: Albertina CM, fol. 19 verso, 20.

1695-1700 Town Palace of Prince Eugene of Savoy in Vienna. E: HA IV/5; D: Würzburg, University Library, so-called 'sketch-book' of Balthasar Neumann.

Before 1696 until 1699 Plan for a Lustgartengebäude (pleasure garden house). Probably carried out without Fischer's knowledge, 1699-1701, at Liblitz (now Liblice, Czechoslovakia). E: HA IV/18; Ds: Milan, Archivio Communale, Raccolta delle Stampe, Domenico Martinelli bequest, vol. IX, fol. 33, Albertina CM, fol. 15 verso, 16, Zagreb, nos. 70, 71.

1696-1707 Kollegienkirche (University Church) in Salzburg (first design 1694). Es: HA IV/9, 10, 11; Ds: Zagreb, nos. 7, 47, 48, 49, 76, Salzburg LA and MCA, Albertina AZ.

1696 until after 1711 Schloss Schönbrunn near Vienna (now Vienna XIII), second project (designs probably before 1696). Es: HA IV/3, 4, P 17; D: Zagreb, no. 73.

1696 Project for the regulation of the Danube near Grein, Lower Austria.

1696 Pilgrimage church of Maria Kirchenthal, near Lofer, Salzburg. Foundation stone laid in 1694, designs submitted 1696.

c. **1696** Design for a monstrance for the Church of Maria Loreto in Prague (attribution). D: at one time in Vienna, Harrach collection; goldsmith's drawings in Prague, archives of monastery of Maria Loreto.

1698-1700 Chapel of Schloss Frain in Moravia, now Vranov nad Dyjí, Czechoslovakia (attribution).

1699-1705 Ursulinenkirche (Ursuline Church) in Salzburg (attribution).

1699 Two triumphal arches for the entry of Joseph I and his bride Wilhelmine Amalie of Brunswick-Lüneburg into Vienna. Es: HA IV/1; engraving by the Augsburg engraver Wolffgang after Johann Bernhard Fischer von Erlach and an anonymous engraving, both in the Historisches Museum of the city of Vienna; D: Prague, Museum of Applied Art.

1699 Design for a festive decoration, perhaps carried out. D: Albertina CM, fol. 15 verso.

Between 1699 and 1702 Design for an 'Indian' or chinoiserie cabinet for Queen Wilhelmine Amalie in the Imperial Palace (Hofburg) in Vienna (carried out, but not preserved).

1699-1706 Palais Batthyány (now Schönborn Palace) in Vienna. E: P 11.

Before 1701 Design for a fountain in Tetschen (Děčin in Czechoslovakia), not carried out. D: Zagreb, no. 57.

1700-1709 Schloss Klesheim near Salzburg. E: HA IV/17; Ds: Zagreb, nos. 50, 51, Albertina CM, fol. 17 verso, 18; a wooden model of the palace, different from Fischer's designs and partly damaged during the Second World War, is in Salzburg MCA.

c. **1700** Plan for a Gartengebäude (garden house), not carried out. E: HA IV/19; Ds: Zagreb, no. 72, Albertina CM, fol. 20 verso, 21a.

1701 *Prospekt des Schlosses Schönbrunn* (View of Schloss Schönbrunn), Vienna. One or more engravings, now missing; a proof of one of them in Karlsruhe, Staatliche Kunsthalle, Collection of Plans.

c. **1702** Design for the high altar of the parish church of Winterberg in Moravia (now Vimperk, Czechoslovakia). Carried out in a different form.

1704 Project for a Lustschloss (garden palace) for Frederick I, King in Prussia (not carried out). Ds: Albertina CM, fol. 23, 23 verso, 24.

1705/6 Wooden Josephssäule (St Joseph's Column) on the Hoher Markt in Vienna (not preserved). Design between 1702 and 1705. E: P 14; engraving by C. Engelbrecht and J. A. Pfeffel, probably after Johann Bernhard Fischer von Erlach.

1705 Designs for the halberds of Joseph I's *Trabantengarde*. D: Vienna, Kunsthistorisches Museum, Waffensammlung.

From 1705 Preliminary work for *Entwurff Einer Historischen Architectur*.

1706 *Castrum doloris* for King Pedro II of Portugal, in Vienna (not handed down in engravings or drawings).

1708/9 Preliminary drawings for a book of engravings showing views of the buildings erected in Salzburg under the patronage of Archbishop Johann Ernst Graf Thun (not published).

After 1708 until 1714 Bohemian Chancellery in Vienna. E: P 13; Ds: Zagreb, nos. 53, 54.

1709 High altar of the Franciscan Church in Salzburg; designed probably in 1708 (attribution). D: Salzburg, archives of the Franciscan monastery.

Between 1709 and 1711 Refashioning of the façade of the Dietrichstein (later Lobkowitz) Palace in Vienna. E: P 7; Ds: at one time in the Harrach collection, Vienna.

c. **1710-15** Villa Huldenberg in Weidlingau near Vienna (now Vienna XIV). Recently demolished. E: P 28; Ds: Albertina CM, fol. 19; Stockholm, National Museum, Collection of Graphic Arts, Tessin-Horleman Collection.

1710-16 (approx.) Gartenpalais Trautson in Vienna, with garden and orangery. Es: HA IV/6, 7, P 21, 22, 23; Ds: Albertina AZ, Zagreb, nos. 58, 59.

1711 *Castrum doloris* for Joseph I in the Augustinian Church in Vienna. E: J. A. Delsenbach after Joseph Emanuel Fischer von Erlach in C. G. Heraeus, *Trauer-Pracht . . . Kayser Josepho I . . . ,* Vienna, 1711; D: Zagreb, no. 79.

1711 *Castrum doloris* for Joseph I in the Cathedral of St Stephen in Vienna. D: Zagreb, no. 78.

1712 Manuscript of Fischer's History of Architecture, *Entwurff Einer Historischen Architectur*, presented to the Emperor Charles VI. Vienna, Österreichische Nationalbibliothek, Handschriftensammlung, Cod. 10791.

c. **1712** Design for the Schwarzenberg Town Palace in Vienna (attribution). Carried out by Joseph Emanuel Fischer von Erlach in a different form from 1722/3, but not preserved. E: P 5; Ds: Albertina AZ.

From 1713 Palais Gallas in Prague. Building began in this year. E: HA IV/8; D: Zagreb, no. 55; cardboard model in Schloss Friedland (now Frýdlant in Czechoslovakia).

Before 1713 Drawings for two engravings in Joseph Emanuel Fischer von Erlach's *Prospekte und Abriße einiger Gebäude von Wien*. E: P 6, 28.

1713 Design for an 'Indian' or chinoiserie cabinet in Schloss Schönbrunn. Carried out, but not preserved.

1714 Sepulchral monument for Johann Wenzel Graf Wratislaw von

Mitrowitz in the Church of St James's in Prague (not completed until 1716). E: HA IV/21; D: Vienna, Graphische Sammlung Albertina, Artaria Collection.

From 1715 Church of St Charles Borromeo (Karlskirche) in Vienna (completed by Joseph Emanuel Fischer von Erlach in 1725; interior decoration and furnishing completed in 1737/8). Es: HA IV/12, 13, 14, 15; Ds: Salzburg MCA, Mauthausen, Upper Austria, private collection.

1715/16 until 1721 Elector's Chapel in Breslau Cathedral (now Wrocław, Poland).

1716 Designs for the festive decorations of the Schwarzenberg Town Palace and of Fischer's house in Vienna on the occasion of the birth of the Archduke Leopold (handed down only in description).

1716 Design for a seated statue of the man of sorrows in a wayside chapel (after the frontispiece of Albrecht Dürer's 'Large Woodcut Passion'). D: at one time in the art trade, now missing.

1716 Project for a building for the imperial academy of science in Vienna (not carried out; designs not preserved).

c. **1716–19** Project for the rebuilding of the Imperial Palace (Hofburg) in Vienna (attribution). Not handed down, but a prior condition for the designs for the Emperor's stables and library.

From 1716 Project for the imperial library (Hofbibliothek) in Vienna (attribution). Carried out by Joseph Emanuel Fischer von Erlach in 1723–37; Es: Salomon Kleiner, *Dilucida Repraesentatio . . . Bibliothecae Caesareae . . .*, Vienna, 1737. Drawings for the second part of this work, which was not published, in Vienna, Österreichische Nationalbibliothek Handschriftensammlung, Cod. Min. 71.

1716–18 Central part of the east wing (great hall and staircase) of the Herzogenburg convent in Lower Austria. D: Augustinerchorherrenstift Herzogenburg, archives.

Between 1718 and 1721 Design for the tower of the convent church of Herzogenburg. The raising of the medieval tower by two storeys was carried out in altered form by Matthäus Munggenast and completed in 1767. D: Graz, Landesmuseum Joanneum, Collection of Graphic Arts.

After 1719 until 1723 Imperial stables (Hofstallungen) in Vienna; completed by Joseph Emanuel Fischer von Erlach. E: HA IV/16.

1720 Design for the high altar of the pilgrimage church of Sallapulka in Lower Austria. Ds: Stift Herzogenburg, archives.

From 1720 Rebuilding of the Schwarzenberg Garden Palace in Vienna; completed by Joseph Emanuel Fischer von Erlach. D: Krumau (now Český Krumlov, Czechoslovakia), archives of the Princes of Schwarzenberg.

1721 First edition of Fischer's 'History of Architecture' (*Entwurff Einer Historischen Architectur*), Vienna. Ds: Zagreb, nos. 1–79; Linz, Oberösterreichisches Landesmuseum; Salzburg MCA.

Index